MW00438542

Held in
Perfect Peace

Held in Perfect Peace

100 Devotions to Calm Your Heart

A Guideposts Devotional

ZONDERVAN BOOKS

Held in Perfect Peace
Copyright © 2023 by Guideposts. All rights reserved.

Requests for information should be addressed to:
Zondervan, *3900 Sparks Dr. SE, Grand Rapids, Michigan 49546*

Zondervan titles may be purchased in bulk for educational, business, fundraising, or sales promotional use. For information, please email SpecialMarkets@Zondervan.com.

ISBN 978-0-310-36686-7 (hardcover)
ISBN 978-0-310-36688-1 (audio)
ISBN 978-0-310-36687-4 (ebook)

Acknowledgments: Every attempt has been made to credit the sources of copyrighted material used in this book. If any such acknowledgment has been inadvertently omitted or miscredited, receipt of such information would be appreciated.

Scripture quotations marked (AMP) are taken from the *Amplified Bible*. Copyright © 2015 by The Lockman Foundation, La Habra, California. All rights reserved. • Scripture quotations marked (CEB) are taken from the *Common English Bible*. Copyright © 2011 by Common English Bible. • Scripture quotations marked (ESV) are taken from the *Holy Bible, English Standard Version*. Copyright © 2001 by Crossway Bibles, a division of Good News Publishers. Used by permission. All rights reserved. • Scripture quotations marked (ICB) are taken from *The Holy Bible, International Children's Bible*. Copyright © 1986, 1988, 1999, 2015 by Tommy Nelson™, a division of Thomas Nelson. Used by permission. • Scripture quotations marked (JPS) are taken from *Tanakh: A New Translation of the Holy Scriptures according to the Traditional Hebrew Text*. Copyright © 1985 by the Jewish Publication Society. All rights reserved. • Scripture quotations marked (KJV) are taken from the *King James Version of the Bible*. • Scripture quotations marked (MSG) are taken from *The Message*. Copyright © 1993, 1994, 1995, 1996, 2000, 2001, 2002 by Eugene H. Peterson. • Scripture quotations marked (NABRE) are taken from *The New American Bible Revised Edition*. Copyright © 2011 by TAN Books. • Scripture quotations marked (NASB) are taken from the *New American Standard Bible*. Copyright © 1960, 1971, 1977, 1995, 2020 by The Lockman Foundation. All rights reserved. • Scripture quotations marked (NIV) are taken from *The Holy Bible, New International Version*. Copyright © 1973, 1978, 1984, 2011 by Biblica, Inc. Used by permission of Zondervan. All rights reserved worldwide. zondervan.com • Scripture quotations marked (NKJV) are taken from *The Holy Bible, New King James Version*. Copyright © 1982 by Thomas Nelson. • Scripture quotations marked (NLT) are taken from the *Holy Bible, New Living Translation*. Copyright © 1996, 2004, 2007 by Tyndale House Foundation. Used by permission of Tyndale House Publishers Inc., Carol Stream, Illinois. All rights reserved. • Scripture quotations marked (NRSV) are taken from the *New Revised Standard Version Bible*. Copyright © 1989 by the Division of Christian Education of the National Council of the Churches of Christ in the United States of America. Used by permission. All rights reserved. • Scripture quotations marked (TLB) are taken from *The Living Bible*. Copyright © 1971 by Tyndale House Publishers, Inc., Carol Stream, Illinois. All rights reserved.

Cover design by Pam Walker, W Design Studio
Interior design by Pam Walker, W Design Studio
Cover photo by Nemeziya / Shutterstock
Typeset by Aptara, Inc.

Printed in the United States of America

22 23 24 25 26 27 28 29 30 31 32 33 /LSC/ 15 14 13 12 11 10 9 8 7 6 5 4 3 2 1

*"The greater the level
of calmness of our mind,
the greater our peace of mind,
the greater our ability to enjoy
a happy and joyful life."*

—DALAI LAMA

Contents

Introduction

A Calm Heart Starts with Faith

SHAWNELLE ELIASEN

From my writing room, I watched my teenage son pull into the drive. Then the most reserved of my five boys bolted from his car toward the front porch. His swimmer-strong legs pumped like pistons. The front door flew open. Breathless, Gabriel stood in the entryway, hair still dripping from practice at the pool. His smile was bold and bright. He rocked heel-to-toe.

"Mom! I asked a girl to prom!"

"Wonderful, Gabriel!" I said. Gabe had made the change from home school to public high school three years before and had yet to attend a dance. "When is prom?"

"That's the kicker," he said. "Saturday."

Kicker indeed.

Gabe left to conquer the contents of the fridge while I slipped into ever-widening stress. My to-do list for the week was long. Two birthday celebrations. Coffee with the mama I mentored. A college event with one son and an end-of-year homeschool event with another. Was there even time for a tux fitting? My shoulders tightened. My hands curled on my keyboard.

Stress.

Sometimes it slips over me like a sweater.

Just before Gabriel's prom surprise, my youngest son, Isaiah, and I had been sitting at our table, a tattered world map stretched before us. I'd home-taught five sons over twenty-two years, but fall would bring change. Isaiah would go to public high school as his brothers had. No more blue-backed lesson planners or yellow Ticonderoga pencils standing September-sharp in a painted tin can. No more days filled with the wild wonder of teaching and training. Of books and boys.

"Soon this map can retire," Isaiah said, running his hands over faded Australia. "It's seen its best days."

Panic pulsed like a heartbeat.

What if I'd seen my best days too?

Try as I may, I can't get past the place of figuring out how to deal with anxiety and stress. Fretting over the known. Fearing the unknown. A yoke I've worn since the fall. Yet I don't want to be bound to responses that cause the body, soul, and mind to crave and cry for relief.

I'm so thankful that Jesus offers peace.

In John 14:27, Jesus took the basin and towel and washed the feet of those who would soon walk sandy soil without Him. But He wouldn't leave his friends alone. Jesus spoke of the Counselor, the Holy Spirit, whom the Father would send in His name. Then He spoke of peace. "Peace I leave with you; my peace I give you. I do not give to you as the world gives. Do not let your hearts be troubled and do not be afraid" (NIV).

There's the true kicker.

Worldly peace requires circumstances to be just right. It demands that many things go well. Optimal situations. The trouble is, peaceful ground shifts and then we find our toes back on the welcome mat of worry.

Jesus's peace is different.

It's steady. Sustaining. It doesn't shift with circumstance. It stretches from this world to eternity. Knowing who He is and trusting His promises offer a soul-anchor. A shoring up of our very foundation. He provides a peace so deeply rooted that in even hard circumstances, our hearts can remain calm. When we surrender to the Lord, to His intervention and care, the Spirit brings peace.

My beloved friend Jalois resides in heaven now, but before she left to worship at the throne, she had peaceful living mastered. "Your heart can be still, Sweetie," she'd say when I'd share trials and tribulations. "The Lord has this." Sometimes when she'd speak, I'd stretch my palms open flat. Jalois didn't live a life free of stress. She just knew where to take it.

The writers of the devotions in *Held in Perfect Peace* want to come alongside you in friendship. To encourage you. To speak God's goodness into anxious places. To share stories of how the Lord has been faithful in their stressful circumstances. It's a coming around the table. A gathering of glory. We'll praise Him together for the great things He has done!

Oh, one last thing. The week before prom was happy and prom night was precious. The Lord provided strength, energy, and even removed a few commitments. I surrendered the stress and lived calmly in the moment. Memories will be forever etched on our hearts.

As for the next chapter of my life, that remains to be written. But each day, I do my best to trust. And I'm growing in peace. I'm learning to live calmly in all moments. To borrow the words of a favorite singer-songwriter, Sara Groves, from her song titled "He's Always Been Faithful":

> Morning by morning, I wake up to find
> The power and comfort of God's hand in mine
> Season by season, I watch Him, amazed
> In awe of the mystery of His perfect ways
> All I have need of, His hand will provide
> He's always been faithful to me.

The Great Trumpet

SABRA CIANCANELLI

*And he shall send his angels with
a great sound of a trumpet, and
they shall gather together.*

MATTHEW 24:31 (KJV)

You know, Mom, trumpets are the loudest instruments," Solomon says. I'm making dinner in the kitchen just off the dining room/music room, and for the last twenty minutes I've been enduring the relentless repetition of the first few bars of the *Rocky* theme.

"I believe it," I answer. Solomon has been playing trumpet for four years now, and we're over the hump on ear-piercing wrong notes. Most of the time I'm in awe that he can create such beautiful music, though there are still moments when I wish he'd chosen something smaller, softer, like the flute or clarinet.

Solomon loves that his instrument is mentioned in the Bible. His eyes light up and a smile comes across his lips whenever he spots *trumpet*, as if it were placed there for him. My understanding of certain scriptures has transformed too. I nod in agreement the way only a mom of a trumpet player can when I come across verses that speak about the trumpet's strength, the way it signifies an alarm of war, a call to assemble, or a symbol of the beginning of deliverance, as in when "the great trumpet will be blown" (Isaiah 27:13, NKJV).

I'm finishing dinner when Solomon moves on to playing a trumpet concerto. In seconds, I feel my mood lift with the music, pure and peaceful, filling every nook of my spirit with heavenly sound.

Let Us Pray

Dear Lord, thank You for the many ways Your Word grows with our lives and in our hearts.

Further Reflection

PSALM 119:105 (KJV)

Thy word is a lamp unto my feet, and a light unto my path.

2 TIMOTHY 3:16–17 (KJV)

All scripture is given by inspiration of God, and is profitable for doctrine, for reproof, for correction, for instruction in righteousness: That the man of God may be perfect, thoroughly furnished unto all good works.

Bedtime Rituals

BROCK KIDD

I will both lay me down in peace, and sleep.

PSALM 4:8 (KJV)

Sleep. The word to me is almost like a poem. When I was a child, bedtime rituals were a sweet prelude to sleep. Poems like Eugene Field's "Wynken, Blynken, and Nod" sent me floating off to dreamland in a wooden shoe, and spoken rituals such as "Night-night," "Sleep tight," and "Sweet dreams" made me snuggle in safety.

When my son, Harrison, came into my life, I wanted to give him a unique bedtime tradition. Singing "Jesus Loves Me" as I tucked him in continued into his middle school years.

Now with two young girls, Mary Katherine and Ella Grace, we've added yet another nighttime custom: programmable pillows! Every night after bedtime stories and prayers, each girl gets her turn. They tell me what they would like to dream, and together we make a big show of programming their pillows for the dreams ahead.

Sleep is a subject of great interest these days. Sleep doctors, sleep clinics, and entire industries have grown around our country's sleeplessness. I wonder if maybe we've strayed away from something simple in this crazy world in which we live.

My mother had a little sign on her bedside table: "God tucks mothers in at night." The truth is, no matter our age or stage in life, we all need someone to tuck us in. Here's another

truth: God, as our Father, vows to be our refuge (Psalm 46:1), gives His angels charge over us (Psalm 91:11), and keeps us from evil (2 Thessalonians 3:3). The list continues through the Bible.

Can sleep really be a poem of peace? Suppose God is standing by, like a Father, waiting to program our pillows with His best promises. Why not call on Him and see what happens?

Let Us Pray

Father, tuck us in at night. Let us rest in Your promises.

Further Reflection

ISAIAH 54:13 (KJV)

And all thy children shall be taught of the LORD; and great shall be the peace of thy children.

Closer to Grace

EDWARD GRINNAN

*Grace and peace be yours in abundance
through the knowledge of God
and of Jesus our Lord.*

2 PETER 1:2 (NIV)

I woke up this morning, my head full of worry. Nothing obvious was at the root of it. Just a generalized angst, pressure in my chest and behind my eyes, the soles of my feet slightly damp, my breathing shallow.

Who isn't stressed out these days? My friend, author and motivational speaker Jon Gordon, claims he's too blessed to be stressed. I wish I could say that.

My stress engine always seems to be idling, waiting for a reason to rev up. Work deadlines, the economy, politics, health issues, or just waiting in line at the grocery store.

Another friend says stress is a fundamental force of nature. Without it, the world would come to a dismal standstill. Nothing would ever get done. Society would crumble. We would be lost. Yep, stress is a great motivator.

But a constant state of stress is harmful. Researchers agree that prolonged stress levels contribute to just about every health condition you can name. That kind of stress is corrosive to the soul. It breaks us down and distances us from grace. Grace and stress are antithetical.

We all need reminders of that. I say the Serenity Prayer. That's what I did this morning. Nothing banishes anxiety like putting the focus on God and concentrating our thoughts on His love for us.

It also helps to have a golden retriever jumping up on your bed first thing in the morning and licking your chin. Did I mention my golden's name? It's Grace.

Let Us Pray

Father, I am quick to worry, to forget Your presence in every moment of my life, in the midst of every challenge and joy. Help me stay out of my own head and remain in Your loving arms.

Further Reflection

JUDE 1:2 (NIV)

Mercy, peace and love be yours in abundance.

ROMANS 12:9–10 (NIV)

Love must be sincere. . . . Be devoted to one another in love. Honor one another above yourselves.

God's Solutions

JOHN DILWORTH

But those who wait on the Lord shall renew their strength; they shall mount up with wings like eagles.

ISAIAH 40:31 (NKJV)

Yesterday, I sorted prayer concerns from a small basket on a bookshelf in the room where I pray. When a difficult problem keeps me from sleeping, I write it down. I place the concern into this basket for God's attention and ask Him to guide me in handling it. Then I wait for His response.

I started this routine a few years ago as I struggled to apply one of Dr. Norman Vincent Peale's teachings from Ephesians 6:13 (NIV) that "after you have done everything, to stand." My shortcoming was not so much in giving up problems but in letting God keep them. My trust was not strong enough "to stand" firm—I regularly took back problems.

However, through this symbolic act of letting go of worries, I can picture the requests in God's in-basket and out of mine. The most significant change I've noticed since using this practice is that I've become content in waiting for God. I have found that with His response also comes renewal, bringing fresh insight, energy, and confidence all in perfect timing to deal with the issue.

As I moved my concerns from the basket into a folder of answered prayers, the practice of reading the old problems that I had taken to God and reflecting with gratitude on His solutions brought a powerful realization of why my trust has grown.

Let Us Pray

Dear Lord, when my trust starts to waver, remind me again to stand awhile. Amen.

Further Reflection

PROVERBS 16:3 (NKJV)

Commit your works to the LORD, And your thoughts will be established.

2 CORINTHIANS 12:9 (NKJV)

And He said to me, "My grace is sufficient for you, for My strength is made perfect in weakness." Therefore most gladly I will rather boast in my infirmities, that the power of Christ may rest upon me.

Blinded by the Light

REBECCA ONDOV

*See, darkness covers the earth and
thick darkness is over the peoples,
but the LORD rises upon you.*

ISAIAH 60:2 (NIV)

The golden glow of dawn crowned the mountain. I drummed my fingers on the steering wheel of the pickup. A cloud of dust swirled behind the horse trailer as I barreled down the dirt road to the trailhead. It'd been a long week at work. My income from my commission-sales job had plummeted because of the downturn in the economy. All the joy had drained out of me, and I viewed myself as a failure. I couldn't wait to unload my horse for an all-day trail ride.

The road meandered through a gully. The truck chugged through the curve and up a steep hill. Suddenly, the sun popped over the mountain. It reflected off the dust on the windshield and blinded me with seven thousand pounds of horse trailer pushing me. Frantically, I grasped the steering wheel and floored the brakes. The truck and trailer skidded to a stop.

I leaned my head backward against the window. My heart pounded. For that fraction of a second, I was blinded to the world. All I could see and think about was the light.

I sighed. *That's what I need to do. God is the Light. Quit feeding on thoughts of failure and focus on His Word.*

I had lost my peace because I'd concentrated on the darkness of failure. But I hadn't failed because I hadn't quit. After my horseback ride, I found encouraging verses in the Bible and meditated on them daily. At work, I expanded in new directions. It wasn't long before I was wrapped in God's peace once again.

Let Us Pray

Lord, thank You for showing me how to persevere by reflecting on You.

Further Reflection

JOHN 8:12 (NIV)

When Jesus spoke again to the people, he said, "I am the light of the world. Whoever follows me will never walk in darkness, but will have the light of life."

Turning Worry into Worship

ERIKA BENTSEN

Have faith in God.

MARK 11:22 (NLT)

It's 2:45 a.m. I make a fist and pound my pillow into shape, but it's no use. Sleep escapes me. Friends think ranch life is carefree and pastoral. It's anything but. Road disputes. Water disputes. Grazing restrictions.

I switch on the light and open my Bible. Israelites enslaved in Egypt. *Nah, not uplifting.* My thumb chooses another spot. Then another. The Israelites keep sinning. The prophets keep warning of total dispersal; only remnants survive. I sigh and close the book. Turmoil has been going on since the dawn of time and doubtless will continue until the end of time. I feel worse.

"Life would be so much better without all the stresses we put on ourselves and each other," I grumble.

The reply was unexpected: *I got them through that. I can get you through this. Believe Me. Trust Me. Follow Me.*

I reconsider the depressing Bible scenes. Though facing seemingly impossible odds, God's people didn't quit. I glance at the clock and feel a thrill. It's 3:16 a.m. I am reminded of John 3:16: "For God so loved the world."

I grab a piece of paper and scribble down ideas for the problems I can do something about. I add notes in the margins about the blessings God bestows on me. At that moment, I turn worry into worship. Peace surrounds me, and I drift off to sleep.

Let Us Pray

Life will never be easy, Lord, but You are there, just as You have been since the dawn of time and will continue to be until the end of time.

Further Reflection

DEUTERONOMY 30:10 (NLT)

The LORD your God will delight in you if you obey his voice and keep the commands and decrees written in this Book of Instruction, and if you turn to the Lord your God with all your heart and soul.

PSALM 22:8 (NLT)

Is this the one who relies on the LORD? Then let the LORD save him! If the LORD loves him so much, let the LORD rescue him!

Releasing to God

SHAWNELLE ELIASEN

Finally, brothers and sisters, rejoice! Strive for full restoration, encourage one another, be of one mind, live in peace. And the God of love and peace will be with you.

2 CORINTHIANS 13:11 (NIV)

We have a trampoline in the yard. Countless kids have jumped on it over the years—friends of our lineup of boys. But on days like today, when the sun is warm and the air is cool, we sit on the trampoline and read.

I read out loud, and my two younger boys stretch out on their backs, arms folded under heads, smiles to the sun. Suddenly, it's too good to pass up. I dog-ear our book and stretch out too. The blue of the sky is rich and deep. There's not a single cloud. I close my eyes and let my face grow warm. Radiance presses past the physical into my soul.

I begin to think about how this golden rest is like the peace of God. The Bible tells us that when we commit to prayer rather than worry, when we present our needs with an offering of thanksgiving, we'll experience God's brand of peace. It's consuming, completing, pure, and like nothing else.

This isn't always easy for me. Often, I struggle and scrap for control. It's then that I cower in the darkness. When I let go, when I open my heart to God, the light comes in.

My boys settle beside me, and my arms cradle their necks. Our breath becomes a rhythm. "We should get back to lessons," I say eventually.

"Five more minutes?" a boy asks.

I kiss their blond heads. They smell of soap and skin that's warmed by the sun. I can't resist. "OK," I say, "we'll stay." I want to rest in this peace.

Let Us Pray

Father, thank You for the sweet, true peace
that is found only in You. Amen.

Further Reflection

PSALM 29:11 (NLT)

The LORD gives his people strength. The LORD blesses them with peace.

ISAIAH 26:12 (NLT)

LORD, you will grant us peace; all we have accomplished is really from you.

Sunset Prayers

ASHLEY KAPPEL

*Let the heavens rejoice, let the earth
be glad; let the sea resound, and all that
is in it. Let the fields be jubilant, and
everything in them; let all the trees
of the forest sing for joy.*

PSALM 96:11–12 (NIV)

It had been a day. You know the kind: spouse out of town, kids wound up from school, dinner taking extralong to get on the table, and bedtime strung out with a few added requests for milk, water, books, and snuggles. The days with two little ones can be so long; I wouldn't trade it for the world, but I do value the few minutes of peace I get when everyone is safely tucked in.

Shutting their doors for (really) the last time, I made my way down the stairs feeling completely discouraged. Olivia's final, unprompted "I love you, Ma" after my terse denial to keep her milk cup in her bed had pretty much broken me.

Suddenly, I heard a huge gush of water. A thunderstorm unloaded gallons of rain on our neighborhood. I rushed to the window, in awe of this midsummer deluge, and that's when I saw it: the most beautiful sunset looming low in my kitchen window.

I have no doubt that God sent me that sunset to remind me that His mercies, like my patience, will be renewed in the morning.

Perhaps foolishly, I marched back upstairs, sneaked into the kids' rooms, and covered their dozing faces with kisses.

Now, when I see a beautiful sunset at that window, I'm reminded that God knows my heart and hears my prayers, even when I forget to say them out loud!

Let Us Pray

God, help me to remember that these precious children are Yours, only on loan to me for a little while, and that sleep always, eventually, comes.

Further Reflection

GENESIS 9:16 (NIV)

Whenever the rainbow appears in the clouds, I will see it and remember the everlasting covenant between God and all living creatures of every kind on the earth.

PSALM 19:1 (NIV)

The heavens declare the glory of God; the skies proclaim the work of his hands.

LAMENTATIONS 3:22–23 (NIV)

Because of the Lord's great love we are not consumed, for his compassions never fail. They are new every morning; great is your faithfulness.

Happiness Is a Haircut

ERIN MacPHERSON

For he will hide me in his shelter
in the day of trouble; he will conceal
me under the cover of his tent;
he will lift me high upon a rock.

PSALM 27:5 (ESV)

Sarah handed me a pair of scissors right as I walked in the front door. "Take a big piece off from wherever you want."

She turned around and showed me other places on her head where huge chunks of hair were missing.

I took a deep breath and closed my eyes. Sarah's smiling face urged me forward. I snipped a large chunk off the top, staring as tufts of brown hair floated to the floor and landed in a pile around her green flip-flops.

I blinked back tears and looked into her eyes, expecting to see anguish. Instead, I saw peace. Pure, God-given peace that seemed to hover in the air, making what would otherwise be a terrible evening one of laughter, of joy even.

She took the scissors out of my hand and gave them to my ten-year-old, who wavered between relishing the idea of being allowed to hack off a chunk of an adult's hair and fear that there would

be repercussions. But there weren't. And his wide eyes turned to laughing eyes as he sheared off what was left of Sarah's bangs.

And so the night progressed, one snip after another, until Sarah's hair was a mottled mess of missing chunks and frazzled tufts. And then came the grand finale: her husband shaved her head.

We all watched and cheered. Sarah laughed. And the torment of what could have been terrible—chemo stealing away my beautiful friend's hair—was replaced by a peace that transcended understanding.

Let Us Pray

Lord, be our peace and joy in otherwise
desperate situations. Amen.

Further Reflection

ISAIAH 41:10 (ESV)

Fear not, for I am with you; be not dismayed, for I am your God; I will strengthen you, I will help you, I will uphold you with my righteous right hand.

Healing from Creation

RHODA BLECKER

There are companions to keep one company, And there is a friend more devoted than a brother.

PROVERBS 18:24 (JPS)

I had purchased an Alex Beattie needlepoint canvas of *The First Day of Creation*, starting it before my husband, Keith, became ill and picking it up again after I began to recover from his death. The beauty of the design helped to heal me, so as soon as I found out that this canvas was the first in a series covering six days of creation, I phoned to purchase the next five. Somehow the idea of re-creating all that splendor gave me a sense of peace.

The person taking my order told me that day six was sold out, and the artist didn't think he would return to the series.

I bought days two, three, four, and five and asked to be put on a list so that if Beattie ever rereleased day six again, I could get it.

The canvases exceeded my expectations. As soon as I finished the first, I began work on the second, which surprised me by being even more beautiful, as if I had never realized that creation became lovelier as it went on. I was sad I would have to stop once I finished the fifth canvas, that I would never finish the series.

I mentioned it to my friend Dawn, who thought about it for a short time and then said, "It's appropriate, really."

"Why?" I asked.

She smiled. "Because creation is really never finished."

Let Us Pray

Thank You, God of creation, for including
friends among Your gifts to us.

Further Reflection

JOB 42:10 (JPS)

And the Lord changed the fortune of Job, when he prayed
for his friends; and the Lord gave Job twice as much as he
had before.

Ready for School

STEPHANIE THOMPSON

I prayed to the LORD, and he answered me.
He freed me from all my fears.

PSALM 34:4 (NLT)

I'm ready to start middle school." Micah held her new backpack filled with notebooks, binders, and a pencil bag.

But I wasn't. My mind churned with apprehension. *Could she find the right classroom when they rotated? Would she remember her locker number? Would she find kind friends? How could she manage the homework? What if she was exposed to peer pressure?*

Maybe I was overprotective and letting my own experiences color how I felt. Growing up, I was the "new kid" at school seven times before I went to college. Walking the halls of Sapulpa Junior High, I felt small and insignificant as I tried to find my classrooms. When I forgot my locker combination, I was too embarrassed to say anything. I lugged around a stack of books for weeks.

Luckily, Micah wasn't shy like me. She knew most of the students in her class. Still, I worried that no one would be there to help her.

The afternoon before the first day of school, another mother emailed me. "Meet tonight in front of the school to pray before the new year begins."

That evening, I circled up with five moms on the sidewalk in front of the middle school building. We closed our eyes. Peace replaced my anxiety as I poured out my fears to God. I wanted my child to be protected and I couldn't be there to do it. But God could. He was more capable than any of us moms.

Micah was ready to start middle school. So was I, thanks to my back-to-school group prayer reminder.

Let Us Pray

Lord, help me to remember that my school assignment is a mother's prayer for her child every day.

Further Reflection

PHILIPPIANS 4:6–7 (NLT)

Don't worry about anything; instead, pray about everything. Tell God what you need, and thank him for all he has done. Then you will experience God's peace, which exceeds anything we can understand. His peace will guard your hearts and minds as you live in Christ Jesus.

Navigating Life

PENNEY SCHWAB

*Rejoicing in hope; patient in tribulation;
continuing instant in prayer.*

ROMANS 12:12 (KJV)

I found the perfect anniversary card for you and Dad," our
daughter Rebecca said. The front featured a man driving and
his wife in the passenger seat. She thinks they are lost. He says
they are not. She wants to ask for directions. He refuses. She
prays silently for strength while he prays silently for patience.
Inside are the words "The couple who prays together stays
together."

My husband, Don, and I have been lost in Baltimore, Dallas,
and other cities too numerous to list. We both have squeaky-
clean driving records but don't trust each other's driving. I
think Don drives too fast. He thinks I drive too slowly. He gets
irritated when I nag because he's speeding or changing lanes
abruptly. I get irritated when he says I'm impeding traffic and
better speed up. But since we like to visit family and friends,
we are stuck with each other. I won't drive in heavy city traffic,
and Don gets sleepy on long stretches of interstate.

We'd argued during a recent trip to Colorado, then spent
an hour hunting for our hotel. We arrived tense and upset, and
it was obvious that traveling together meant we would have to
make some changes. The next day, we bought a navigation system

with maps and clear verbal instructions, best route, and construction information. Don has slowed down (most of the time), and I'm trying to remain calm and silent. I'm keeping pace with traffic (most of the time), and Don isn't urging me to speed up. We're traveling—and praying—with more trust and peace.

Let Us Pray

Dear Lord, thank You for a husband who prays with me and for me, even when he prays for patience while I'm praying for strength.

Further Reflection

PSALM 19:14 (KJV)

Let the words of my mouth, and the meditation of my heart, be acceptable in thy sight, O Lord, my strength, and my redeemer.

MATTHEW 18:20 (KJV)

For where two or three are gathered together in my name, there am I in the midst of them.

Be Still

LOGAN ELIASEN

Be still, and know that I am God.

PSALM 46:10 (KJV)

I slid into the driver's seat and checked the clock—five minutes behind schedule. I might still make it to class on time if I didn't hit any red lights. I pulled out onto the road; it was packed solid.

As I joined the ranks of unmoving vehicles, I could feel my heart thumping. I glanced at my mirror, and my reflection stared back with shadowed eyes. I looked as if I hadn't slept in days, which was accurate.

Law school was difficult. My days were crammed with intricate assignments and dense casebooks. At night, I couldn't shut off my mind. My brain kept trying to connect statutes and cases while I tossed back and forth.

I looked out at the line of brake lights and drummed my fingers on the steering wheel. What a waste of time! I could be skimming my notes or working on tomorrow's readings. Instead, I was forced to sit here, forced to be still.

I ran a thumb over my stubbly cheek. When had I last taken the time to be still? When had I last rested in God's strength?

I steadied my breathing and cleared my mind of all the work I had to do. It could wait. In the busyness, I had forgotten that though I am just Logan, God is God. These burdens were too heavy for me but not for Him. Remembering that lifted some of the pressure off my chest.

The van in front of me began to move forward, and I eased off the brake. I knew I was driving toward a full day, but that moment of stillness anchored me in the One who would get me through it.

Let Us Pray

Lord, show me Your peace when I am restless.

Further Reflection

MATTHEW 11:28–30 (NIV)

Come to me, all you who are weary and burdened, and I will give you rest. Take my yoke upon you and learn from me, for I am gentle and humble in heart, and you will find rest for your souls. For my yoke is easy and my burden is light.

Escape to the Mountains

GAIL THORELL SCHILLING

When my heart is overwhelmed: lead me to the rock that is higher than I.

PSALM 61:2 (KJV)

When I need to clear my mind, find perspective, or just escape wearying routine, I head for the hills. Luckily, White Mountain National Forest is just an hour north of my home. From several overlooks, I ponder the reassuring bulk of Cannon Mountain, a granite dome 4,080 feet high. Even from a distance, the mountain helps me to feel secure and calm.

If I visit midweek, tourists are fewer and my expedition feels more spiritual than recreational. A fifteen-minute ride on the aerial tramway to the summit exposes me to a panoramic vista of three states and Quebec and weather drastically different from the base. On a mild autumn day, for example, a snow squall may blast me on the observation deck. Even on a pretty June afternoon, the temperature can drop 20 degrees at the summit.

Yet here, so high up the mountain that cars in the parking lot below look like specks, peace returns, even as manic wind tears at my clothes and lashes out at my hair. Perhaps it's just the altitude or escaping distractions that I find so soothing. After all, even Jesus needed time apart.

I learned the security of high ground from hiking with pack goats in the Rocky Mountains. These obliging, social creatures followed us, carrying our gear in mini panniers. When we camped at night, however, the goats instinctively sought the highest ground for protection against predators.

Like the goats, I eventually need to descend the mountain and return to daily life and all its niggling anxieties and obligations. Mountaintop getaways keep me grounded.

Let Us Pray

Lord, thank You for the ways Your creation refreshes our souls.

Further Reflection

MARK 6:31 (KJV)

And he said unto them, Come ye yourselves apart into a desert place, and rest a while: for there were many coming and going, and they had no leisure so much as to eat.

LUKE 6:12–13 (KJV)

And it came to pass in those days, that he went out into a mountain to pray, and continued all night in prayer to God. And when it was day, he called unto him his disciples: and of them he chose twelve, whom also he named apostles.

An Early Start

MARILYN TURK

Satisfy us in the morning with your unfailing love, that we may sing for joy and be glad all our days.

PSALM 90:14 (NIV)

I slap the alarm button before the noise wakes my husband. Forcing myself out of bed, I stumble through the house, following the cat whose meow demands food, silencing him before he wakes my grandson.

Going through the motions of my routine, I'm like a toy robot whose batteries are running down. I stare through the kitchen window as the coffee brews.

I am definitely not a morning person. But I made a commitment years ago to spend time with God before my day got started. The only way to find the time was to get up earlier, before anyone else did. As a result, my life became more peaceful.

It still wasn't easy, and often I battled with my self-will to maintain the routine.

Clutching a cup of coffee, I sit at the table, then open my devotional book and journal. The house is quiet, and the solitude alarms me. "Lord, are You awake yet? Did You remember our appointment?"

I feel someone looking at me and glance toward the hallway to see if my grandson has sneaked up on me. But no one's there.

Then I look toward our sliding glass door to the backyard and I see him: Mr. Squirrel. He (or maybe she) is a squirrel we've been feeding for several years. He's become so familiar with us that he will take a peanut out of our hands.

I smile because he knew I would be there, and he was waiting patiently for me to give him my attention. Just like God.

Let Us Pray

Lord, thank You for the smile You gave me this early morning and for always waiting patiently for my attention.

Further Reflection

PSALM 5:3 (NIV)

In the morning, LORD, you hear my voice; in the morning I lay my requests before you and wait expectantly.

PSALM 65:8 (NIV)

The whole earth is filled with awe at your wonders; where morning dawns, where evening fades, you call forth songs of joy.

PSALM 143:8 (NIV)

Let the morning bring me word of your unfailing love, for I have put my trust in you. Show me the way I should go, for to you I entrust my life.

The Perfect Present

SABRA CIANCANELLI

Whoever is patient has
great understanding.

PROVERBS 14:29 (NIV)

*T*icktock. Putting away the dishes, I notice the sound of the cuckoo clock beside me. After the long summer vacation, we had another challenging morning, which proved to be an exercise in patience. Finding backpacks, packing lunch boxes, and remembering homework were all habits we'd easily cast aside, and now we found ourselves stressed, simply trying to get back into the routine.

This morning, one of Henry's library books went missing, and a frantic search left the living room a mess, couch cushions misplaced, the contents from the shelf beneath the coffee table spread out on the carpet. All that chaos, and the book was exactly where it should have been—tucked safely in his backpack.

Ticktock, and the maiden on a swing goes back and forth. It was over a decade ago when I spotted the small clock in a shop window while we were on vacation in Vermont. I mentioned to my husband how I adored it, but the store was closed and we were only visiting the town for a day, so I forgot all about it until my birthday months later. And there it was—the cuckoo clock.

Tony explained how he went back to the store later that day without my noticing. I was amazed at his patience. How had he kept this great gift a secret? So unlike me—I can't wait to share a perfect present, and here he'd managed to save it for just the right time.

Ticktock. I feel myself shift from stressed to blessed.

Let Us Pray

Dear Lord, when the chaos of family life overwhelms me, guide me to my blessings and help me to remember that love is patient.

Further Reflection

ROMANS 8:25 (NIV)

But if we hope for what we do not yet have, we wait for it patiently.

GALATIANS 6:9 (NIV)

Let us not become weary in doing good, for at the proper time we will reap a harvest if we do not give up.

Right Rain

JIM HINCH

Here is my servant, whom I uphold, my chosen, in whom my soul delights.

ISAIAH 42:1 (NRSV)

Sometimes everything is just right. Now it was the rain that was right.

We were on our way home from a trip to Maine, where friends from church had invited us to stay at their small cabin on a lake. It had been a glorious few days. Kayaking. Canoeing. Bike rides. A day trip to the coast to see a lighthouse. Dinners outside and s'mores around a small campfire. The haunting calls of loons at night.

We were sad to go home, not looking forward to the gritty city. But then it began to rain. It rained harder and harder, pelting our car. Our spirits had been flagging, but we all grinned as the rain drummed on the roof and sent up fountains of spray from the highway.

"Let's keep reading," I said to the kids. I'd been reading to them while Kate drove. Suddenly, the car became cozy and

warm as the story unfolded with the rain hammering outside. It was almost as if we were on our own screened porch, safe and dry, listening contentedly to the sound of falling water.

"Look!" cried Benji. We turned and saw, through a distant parting of the storm, not one but two rainbows. They stood out starkly against the dark clouds nearer to us.

Every last trace of sadness was gone now. What could be more perfect than a good story on a rainy day, graced by a double rainbow? What an unexpected gift. We should have expected it from the Giver who never tires of delighting those who seek Him.

Let Us Pray

Lord, help me always to be open to the unexpected ways in which You show me how much You love me.

Further Reflection

EPHESIANS 3:17, 19 (NRSV)

And that Christ may dwell in your hearts through faith, as you are being rooted and grounded in love. And to know the love of Christ that surpasses knowledge, so that you may be filled with all the fullness of God.

1 JOHN 4:16 (NRSV)

So we have known and believe the love that God has for us. God is love, and those who abide in love abide in God, and God abides in them.

No "Worry Prayers"

JON SWEENEY

*So be content with who you are,
and don't put on airs. God's strong
hand is on you; he'll promote you at
the right time. Live carefree before
God; he is most careful with you.*

1 PETER 5:6–7 (MSG)

I think I can almost see God from here as I lie on my back in this grassy field. I have given myself twenty minutes to remain here, to simply lie here and do nothing of any value whatsoever.

Please don't tell my employer; it's the middle of the work-day. Please don't look at the floors in my house that I'm supposed to be vacuuming. Email? Phone? I have left those devices in my office. They may be dinging and ringing; I don't know. There's the dog, too, probably waiting to be walked. Never mind. Not now. Things will get done later.

I hear a bird. Wait; I hear two. And now I see them flitting back and forth. Are they talking with each other? *Kee-kaw, kee-kaw.*

I've been here awhile. I know because an inchworm has made it onto my pants leg. It is the color of the grass. How many others like it are all around me that I cannot see?

This day—this quiet moment of twenty minutes lying in the grass—I will pray for small creatures such as this inchworm, songbirds, and me. I'm too relaxed to worry. There are no "worry prayers" coming from me on this day, at this moment—only thanks for what has been given.

Let Us Pray

For the very gift of life today, I thank You, God.

Further Reflection

PSALM 150:1, 3–6 (NIV)

Praise the LORD. Praise him with the sounding of the trumpet, praise him with the harp and lyre, praise him with timbrel and dancing, praise him with the strings and pipe, praise him with the clash of cymbals, praise him with resounding cymbals. Let everything that has breath praise the LORD.

Safe with God

PENNEY SCHWAB

See, I have tattooed your name
upon my palm.

ISAIAH 49:16 (TLB)

We'd had a fun-packed weekend with our grandchildren
Olivia and Caden and our great-nephews Derek and
Dominick. Tuesday morning, I felt unwell, but I thought I was
just tired. By suppertime, though, I was in too much pain to
eat. At four o'clock Wednesday morning, my husband, Don,
drove me to the emergency room. Five hours, three doctors,
and multiple tests later, I was in the ICU, where I received
antibiotics and pain medications while waiting for a surgeon to
review test results.

It was late afternoon before the surgeon finished his scheduled procedures and examined me. He was "98 percent sure"
it was appendicitis; it was. The surgery was uneventful and my
recovery smooth. The only thing that wasn't routine was my attitude. I usually have a problem with letting go and letting God.

From the time I walked through the hospital door until my
release, I didn't have a single moment of panic, fear, or worry. I
didn't care that I met the surgeon less than one hour before he
operated or that I hadn't checked the credentials of the nurses
who managed my IVs. I trusted them to provide everything I
needed for a full recovery.

Now, when a worry pops up, I take a deep breath and remember that experience. I was safe with people I didn't know. Why wouldn't I be far safer with my heavenly Father, who has my name written on the palm of His hand?

Let Us Pray

Lord, I would place my hand in Thine, nor
ever murmur nor repine; content, whatever lot
I see, since 'tis my God that leadeth me.
("He Leadeth Me" by Joseph H. Gilmore)

Further Reflection

LUKE 12:6–7 (TLB)

What is the price of five sparrows? A couple of pennies? Not much more than that. Yet God does not forget a single one of them. And he knows the number of hairs on your head! Never fear, you are far more valuable to him than a whole flock of sparrows.

Take a Time-Out

GAIL THORELL SCHILLING

[Jesus] said to them, "Come with me by yourselves to a quiet place and get some rest."

MARK 6:31 (NIV)

My daughter Trina tried to work baby Julia's arm into the narrow sleeve of the soft aqua sweater I had knit for her. It didn't fit. Ever gracious, Trina suggested, "Let's take a picture, even of one arm!" She knew I'd worked for months on this so-called easy beginner pattern. I knitted the panels well but had assembled them wrong. These skinny sleeves would not accommodate a toothbrush, much less a newborn's arms. My creation was a dud. The matching hat matched all right. It sported holes from dropped stitches and other mistakes. Another dud.

Despite my frustration, I knew enough to unravel the garments in their entirety and reuse the fingerling wool. This took time and produced yarn that looked like a kinky mass of ramen noodles. My knitter friends, however, had taught me the secret of reclamation: soak the kinky yarn in a wash solution to relax the fibers. This, too, took time—about thirty minutes. Next, the wet yarn had to be blotted and allowed to air-dry for several hours. More time. Whatever angst I felt at my failures dissipated as the day wore on.

Yet again, my fiber arts were teaching me lessons in humility and patience. Plans might not work out; our best efforts can unravel. Like my yarn, sometimes I just need time to unkink, soak up peace, and rest. It's reassuring to know even Jesus sometimes needed to take time out for rest.

Let Us Pray

Lord, You teach me profound truths in such simple ways. Thank You.

Further Reflection

PSALM 46:10 (NIV)

He says, "Be still, and know that I am God; I will be exalted among the nations, I will be exalted in the earth."

ISAIAH 30:15 (NIV)

This is what the Sovereign LORD, the Holy One of Israel, says: "In repentance and rest is your salvation, in quietness and trust is your strength, but you would have none of it."

I Lift My Heart

JULIA ATTAWAY

*Let us lift up our hearts and
our hands to God in heaven.*

LAMENTATIONS 3:41 (NIV)

My usual ability to slog through adversity wasn't working. Weariness over family difficulties had mixed itself up with sadness, and the two crashed over me in wave after wave. I sat in church, stuck in my sad funk, while the service moved forward.

I had no idea how to make anything better in my life. I praised God with my lips because I knew how to do that. I stood up, sat down, and knelt at the right times because I could do that as well. But I only half-listened to the sermon.

By the time we were encouraged to "Lift up your hearts," instead of responding, "We lift them up to the Lord," I muttered, "No! You do it!" *You gave me emotions, Lord,* I pouted. *If You want me to figure this out, You're going to have to unclog my heart.*

I reached into my purse for tissues, suddenly needing them. Tears washed away the aching question of what to do, and I thought instead about what kind of person I want to be. Mess or no mess, I am the Lord's. Sure, I'd rather draw near to Him with a quiet heart and peaceful life, but since that apparently wasn't an option right now, I would have to serve Him in the midst of my situation. I took a deep breath and lifted my heart to God, giving it to Him as if for the first time.

"Go in peace to love and serve the Lord," the pastor said.

"Thanks be to God," I replied ... and meant it.

Let Us Pray

Jesus, I would rather be happy today. But if
I cannot be, I know that I am Yours always.

Further Reflection

PHILIPPIANS 3:20 (NIV)

But our citizenship is in heaven. And we eagerly await a Savior from there, the Lord Jesus Christ.

The Minimum

JEFF CHU

Observe my Sabbaths and have reverence for my sanctuary. I am the LORD.

LEVITICUS 26:2 (NIV)

We all need rest. Our bodies and minds need it. While scientists still don't fully understand the mechanisms of sleep, they have proved that when we're well rested, we think better, we learn better, and we work better.

So one of the things that delighted me when I arrived at the magazine where I currently work was an unusual line in the employee manual: the company "encourages every employee to take a minimum of three weeks' paid vacation." A minimum— not a maximum. It was such a neat variation on the message that you usually hear.

Our spiritual lives are no different from our professional lives—and in some ways, it's even more crucial that we think of minimums, not maximums. In the Bible—the employee manual that God drafted for us—God lays down the minimum, setting aside the Sabbath, which even He took, according to the Creation story. And yet we often fail to abide by that thoughtful recommendation, seeing rest as a luxury, not a necessity.

In God's instructions for healthy living—and in His example—God has given us clear signals: We shouldn't be taking as little time off as we can. We should be taking at least as much time off as we need. Who else would know better than the One who made us?

Let Us Pray

Lord, help me to follow Your holy employee manual, knowing when to work and when to rest.

Further Reflection

HEBREWS 4:9–10 (NIV)

There remains, then, a Sabbath-rest for the people of God; for anyone who enters God's rest also rests from their works, just as God did from his.

1 KINGS 5:4 (NIV)

But now the LORD my God has given me rest on every side, and there is no adversary or disaster.

Escape the Noise

NATALIE PERKINS

The LORD is my shepherd, I shall not want. He makes me lie down in green pastures; he leads me beside still waters; he restores my soul.

PSALM 23:1–3 (NRSV)

"It's quiet," Jan exclaimed. "Thank You, Jesus." My housemates and I often observed how much noisier it seemed here on this beautiful resort island than back home in New York City, which is known as "the city that never sleeps."

We were all there for a two-month contract, and as performers, we had schedules much different than a regular nine-to-five. The noise of lawn maintenance at 9:00 a.m. on our single day off each week—Monday—resulted in grumpy actors and not-so-silent protests for an end to all lawn mowers.

We also found other ways to deal with the discomforts of being away from the familiar. I had shipped my scooter to myself before leaving and took a great deal of delight in scooting to work every day. As part of my daily show warmup, I put in my earbuds, unfolded my scooter, and pushed myself the almost two miles to the theater, following the bike trail and belting along with the R&B divas who sang in my ears. I might have disrupted the golf game of more than a few golfers,

but they all greeted my gaze with smiles and waves. The wind caressed my face, the warmth of the sun kissed my arms, and the trees and flowers all bowed a sweet hello. And for thirty minutes of my day, I had my own private heavenly escape.

Let Us Pray

Creator, what a blessing to experience Your creation every day! I pray for an awareness that allows me to always seek solace, comfort, and peace in what You have placed all around me. Thank You, Holy One, for these gifts here on earth. Amen.

Further Reflection

ISAIAH 55:12 (NRSV)

For you shall go out in joy, and be led back in peace; the mountains and the hills before you shall burst into song, and all the trees of the field shall clap their hands.

MATTHEW 6:1 (NRSV)

Beware of practicing your piety before others in order to be seen by them; for then you have no reward from your Father in heaven.

Letting Go of Fear

DESIREE COLE

Take my yoke upon you and learn from me, for I am gentle and humble in heart, and you will find rest for your souls.

MATTHEW 11:29 (NIV)

The thunder started with a small rumble, but the shaking of the house only grew stronger as the seconds passed. I was rocking my four-month-old son back to sleep after he woke at 1:00 a.m. His eyes were starting to close, his grip around my finger loosening, and he slipped into a deep sleep. I couldn't bear to put him back into bed yet.

Since he was born, I haven't wanted to miss a second of his life, even when I was running on no sleep.

The walls quaked again as I looked over at a small salt lamp plugged into his wall. It furnished the room with an orange glow, which was cast across his cheek. Something about that orange hue caused me to really gaze at my son. Here was this

tiny boy, who often fought sleep as much as I did, now in my arms, dreaming with a small grin.

The scene brought me back to a dream I'd had earlier in the week. I was in a cabin with a woodstove burning in one corner of the room. It created that same orange glow. I wandered around the cabin, exhausted from the weight of my thoughts these days: frightened my son was going to forget me if I was gone for too many minutes; fearful I'd do something wrong that I should have learned before he arrived; embarrassed by my failure to breastfeed. In the dream, my eyes met with Jesus's tender gaze and I stopped moving. "It's time to let go of all this fear by giving it to Me. It won't let you rest, but I will."

Let Us Pray

Jesus, show me when I'm carrying too much.
Help me to keep handing my burdens over to You.
And help me to find rest for my weary soul.

Further Reflection

PSALM 23:2 (NIV)

He makes me lie down in green pastures, he leads me beside quiet waters.

JEREMIAH 31:2 (NIV)

This is what the LORD says: "The people who survive the sword will find favor in the wilderness; I will come to give rest to Israel."

Peaceful Mistakes

LYNNE HARTKE

*Let the peace of Christ rule in
your hearts.*

COLOSSIANS 3:15 (NIV)

I lowered my head into the palm of my hand as the young soloist forgot the entry to the second verse of her song. *What else could go wrong?* I was so excited when my friend Kathy agreed to visit our church, but now I was embarrassed. *Why did she come on this Sunday of all days?*

The morning was one mishap after another. First, the air-conditioning had come on, instead of the necessary heat to ward off the winter chill. Second, the opening video failed to play, upsetting the plans of the worship team. Then the words were incorrect for a worship song in English and Spanish. The video tech had typed *pastry* instead of *paz* (for "peace") and *Joe* instead of *Jesus.*

The soloist was the final straw. I knew my friend would never come again. After the service, I approached Kathy with an apology.

She met me with a smile. She couldn't stop talking about the good humor of the congregation in the midst of minor mishaps and how everyone had cheered on the young soloist.

"My heart was encouraged as the pastor shared the message about peace," she continued. "I've been so worried about my daughter in Paris after the terrorist attacks in Europe."

"But Joe's pastry," I began.

"Peace," she corrected me with a laugh. "I only saw the peace."

Let Us Pray

Open my heart, Lord, to choose peace in the midst of small inconveniences and major concerns.

Further Reflection

PHILIPPIANS 4:6–8 (NIV)

Do not be anxious about anything, but in every situation, by prayer and petition, with thanksgiving, present your requests to God. And the peace of God, which transcends all understanding, will guard your hearts and your minds in Christ Jesus. Finally, brothers and sisters, whatever is true, whatever is noble, whatever is right, whatever is pure, whatever is lovely, whatever is admirable—if anything is excellent or praiseworthy—think about such things.

Green Tomatoes

REBECCA ONDOV

You will keep in perfect peace all who trust in you, all whose thoughts are fixed on you!

ISAIAH 26:3 (NLT)

I stood on my lawn and lobbed the bright green tennis ball for Sunrise, my golden retriever. While she raced away, my thoughts drifted to a situation where I felt I'd been wronged. *God, they never should have done that!* Over the past couple of days, I played the memory over and over in my head until it became a menacing movie. Worse still, I lost my peace.

With the ball in her mouth, Sunrise galloped back, handed it to me, then shifted her weight side to side with her eyes fixed on the ball. I winged it—hard. Sunrise was hot after it, and I grimaced as I watched the ball settle among my tomato plants. She dove into the garden and chomped down with gusto. When she turned around, I saw that, instead of the ball, she had a green tomato in her mouth. Suddenly, she stopped midstride, puckered her brows, and spit it out. Then she stalked around the tomato, cocking her head and making faces at it.

I chuckled as I walked toward her. "Tomatoes might look like a ball, but dogs aren't supposed to bite into them." When those words spilled out of my mouth, instantly I thought, *And bad memories are like green tomatoes. Don't bite them!*

By choosing to continually replay the movie of being hurt, I was wasting my brain space and creating torment.

I picked up the green tomato and threw it in the trash can, along with the bad memory.

Let Us Pray

Thank You, Lord, for free will. Help me to make choices that bring me closer to You. Amen.

Further Reflection

DEUTERONOMY 30:19 (NLT)

Today I have given you the choice between life and death, between blessings and curses. Now I call on heaven and earth to witness the choice you make. Oh, that you would choose life, so that you and your descendants might live!

AMOS 5:15 (NLT)

Hate evil and love what is good; turn your courts into true halls of justice. Perhaps even yet the LORD God of Heaven's Armies will have mercy on the remnant of his people.

Trinket or Treasure?

VICKI KUYPER

Abram left Haran as the Lord had told him. . . . Abram took his wife Sarai, his nephew Lot and everything they owned.

GENESIS 12:4–5 (ICB)

The road sign flashed a warning: Freeway Closed Ahead. We were just a few hundred miles into our eight-hundred-mile journey, and now we'd add a seventy-five-mile detour . . . on a two-lane road . . . through no-man's land . . . following a U-Haul. Lovely. If rolling your eyes while operating a vehicle is an unsafe driving practice, I should have turned on my hazard lights.

But I could only keep driving. Besides, my son was driving the U-Haul, which was filled with my stuff. As I stared at the same truck bumper mile after tedious mile, two thoughts repeatedly ran through my mind: *Why do I own this much junk?* and *The only thing of any value in that truck is the one driving it.*

There's nothing like packing up everything you own to make you realize how much you really have. Sure, in my new home I could use a bed to sleep in, clothes to keep me warm, a few dishes to eat off of, and a chair to sit on. But what about all my "treasures"? The shells I've collected from all over the world? The cast-iron mermaid? The piranha head I brought home after staying in a survival camp in the Amazon?

These were just trinkets that commemorate happy memories. My son, Ryan, was the only true treasure to me and to God. When I later unpacked my boxes and found the tail feathers broken off my favorite ceramic bird statue (the one wearing red tennis shoes), I wasn't heartbroken in the slightest. Instead, I thanked God that my son and I had arrived safely, all in one piece.

Let Us Pray

Dear Lord, help me treasure what You treasure—people, not things. Teach me how to be content with what I have instead of indulging my desire for "more."

Further Reflection

LUKE 12:33–34 (ICB)

Sell the things you have and give to the poor. Get for yourselves purses that don't wear out. Get the treasure in heaven that never runs out. Thieves can't steal it in heaven, and moths can't destroy it. Your heart will be where your treasure is.

Prayer at a Red Light

MARION BOND WEST

Are you tired? Worn out? Burned out on religion? Come to me. Get away with me and you'll recover your life. I'll show you how to take a real rest.

MATTHEW 11:28 (MSG)

I don't like to wait for anything. I have a habit of praying when I have to stop at a red light. It makes the time go by faster. Sometimes I pray for the people in the cars around me or crossing the street. Several times, I've offered prayers on behalf of homeless people. Once I prayed for a dog that appeared lost.

But this day, I had no prayers to offer for others. Instead, I needed prayer. I was tired physically because of health problems and age, feeling overwhelmed and depressed. I whispered a very familiar Bible verse, but God seemed to stop me and suggest a new way to pray it.

Come: "Yes, come on. Move toward Me."

Unto me: "Only to Me; there's no other way."

All ye: "It's not only you, Marion. So many are hurting."

That labor: "Physically, mentally, spiritually."

And are heavy laden: "You don't realize the burdens others carry."

And I: "I. The Great I Am. Look unto Me."

Will give: "Gladly give. I have so much to offer you. You don't have to beg or manipulate. I love to give My children good gifts."

You: "Yes, dear one—you. My beloved. As though you were My only child."

Rest: "For your body and soul. Blessed peace in your thoughts. Rest now, child."

I took a deep breath, and as the light turned green, I left behind the sharp, accusing thought: you think God speaks to you at red lights?

Let Us Pray

Oh, Father, help me keep my faith childlike.

Further Reflection

MARK 6:31 (MSG)

The apostles then rendezvoused with Jesus and reported on all that they had done and taught. Jesus said, "Come off by yourselves; let's take a break and get a little rest." For there was constant coming and going. They didn't even have time to eat.

PSALM 55:6 (MSG)

"Who will give me wings," I ask—"wings like a dove?" Get me out of here on dove wings; I want some peace and quiet.

Uphill Both Ways

BUCK STORM

You will make known to me the path of life;
In Your presence is fullness of joy; In Your
right hand there are pleasures forever.

PSALM 16:11 (NASB)

Remember your grandfather's sob story? Walking to school through the snow? I think every grandfather in America must have attended the same place—certainly they all walked the same route.

As a youngster, I highly suspected my old grandpa was stretching the truth, at least about the snow, since he was from Tempe, Arizona. Now, with a few (OK, more than a few) gray hairs of my own, I'm rethinking. You see, my wife and I spend a lot of time cycling, and on this morning's ride, I began to wonder if there might have been more than a little truth to Grandpa's tale. It certainly felt uphill—both ways. Cycling is like that. Ten minutes of climbing, thirty seconds of zooming down, and then straight back to the grind.

It hit me, about halfway up what felt like my eight-hundredth hill: isn't this exactly like life? I zip through the peaceful stretches without a thought—they're often short-lived—then, legs aching, I'm climbing again, feeling sure I have an invisible plow chained behind my bike.

But there's a funny thing about hills—they get easier the more we ride them. As our tires reel in miles, our faith, like our legs, gets stronger. Because it's on those impossible life-climbs, the ones where we can't see the top, that our miraculous God shows Himself strong. Cheering and coaching, He loves us to the top. And if we take the time to pause and look back, we usually see we weren't the ones doing the pedaling at all.

Life's path gets dark and steep, certainly. But every crank of the pedal builds faith. And faith is measured in one of those beautiful God equations—the bigger it gets, the lighter it is to carry.

Let Us Pray

**Thank You, Lord, for the wind at my back.
I am weak, but You are strong!**

Further Reflection

DEUTERONOMY 31:6 (NASB)

Be strong and courageous, do not be afraid or in dread of them, for the LORD your God is the One who is going with you. He will not desert you or abandon you.

PSALM 91:14, 16 (NASB)

Because he has loved Me, I will save him; I will set him *securely* on high, because he has known My name. I will satisfy him with a long life, And show him My salvation.

A Special Place

KIM TAYLOR HENRY

Peace I leave with you; my peace I give you.

JOHN 14:27 (NIV)

There's a bench on a hillside by my home where I go, especially when I'm seeking comfort and peace, to talk to Jesus. I call it my "special place." From that spot I can see Pikes Peak in the distance, stately behind rolling hills, expanse of fields, and groves of trees. Sitting with Him, surrounded by nature, I feel peace.

The greatest delight of my trip to Israel was when I felt Jesus showing me His "special place" by the Sea of Galilee. Surely, this locale where Jesus chose to concentrate his ministry must have brought Him peace as well. It is called a sea, so I don't know why I pictured it as a small lake, but when I saw its size, its intense-green rock-strewn hillsides splattered with canary-yellow mustard plants, and its surrounding mountain silhouettes, I was mesmerized.

By the rocky shoreline is where it's said Jesus appeared to His disciples after His resurrection. I wandered from our tour group to a place of solitude on a rock by the edge of the sea. Sunlight shimmered on its surface. Transparent water lapped its shoreline. I understood why Christ selected this spot to appear to them. It was, no doubt, part of His "special place"—the sea, the hillsides, the land, the mountains, the peace. After the torture of His execution and the miracle of His resurrection,

Christ didn't choose to return to the masses in Jerusalem or to the barrenness of the desert, but to this familiar spot. I could picture His tender smile as He stood watching His hapless disciples, telling them where to cast their nets, calmly cooking fish as they returned with their huge catch and recognized their Lord.

During and following times of trial, I choose to go to my special place. It felt good to know that Jesus had one too.

Let Us Pray

Lord Jesus, thank You for the peace of special places.

Further Reflection

MATTHEW 15:29 (NIV)

Jesus left there and went along the Sea of Galilee. Then he went up on a mountainside and sat down.

JOHN 21:4 (NIV)

Early in the morning, Jesus stood on the shore, but the disciples did not realize that it was Jesus.

A One-Room Sanctuary

KAREN VALENTIN

When day came, Jesus left and went to a secluded place; and the crowds were searching for Him.

LUKE 4:42 (NASB)

The one bedroom in our apartment has always belonged to my sons. I made it the perfect room for two little boys. I painted the wooden loft bed to look like a tree house and hung Christmas tree lights and a swing underneath. Every inch of the room was dedicated to them as a sanctuary of childhood in which to play and grow. At night, I'd lie down on the couch or the extra futon in their room. I didn't have a space of my own but convinced myself it wasn't necessary.

Years later, I had an extra room built. It was mainly for my parents during their extended visits. The builders came and up went the walls. I walked into the room, shut the door, and sat

in the middle of the floor. There was silence. I couldn't remember the last time I felt this peaceful in my home. I moved the extra futon into the new room, painted the walls a soothing grayish blue, put up expensive curtains, and painted a white Moroccan decal on the walls. I bought beautiful flowers and scented candles.

"Go to your own room," I'd tell the boys when I'd find them playing on my bed with the fluffy, new quilt. When my parents came for their visit, they were content to sleep on the pullout in the living room. I was content not to argue.

I didn't realize how much I needed a place to retreat, breathe, and recharge, but I'm grateful I discovered the importance of sanctuary within those four wonderful walls.

Let Us Pray

Lord, as I serve others and live out my purpose,
help me to find sanctuary and rest in You.

Further Reflection

MATTHEW 6:6 (NASB)

But as for you, when you pray, go into your inner room, close your door, and pray to your Father who is in secret; and your Father who sees what is done in secret will reward you.

MARK 1:35 (NASB)

And in the early morning, while it was still dark, Jesus got up, left the house, and went away to a secluded place, and prayed there for a time.

A Hopeful Move

AMY EDDINGS

My life is deprived of peace, I have forgotten what happiness is; my enduring hope, I said, has perished before the LORD.

LAMENTATIONS 3:17–18 (NABRE)

My husband, Mark, is inventorying all his losses as we plan for our upcoming move. He is not happy. "I have to sell my home and my car. I'm losing my motorcycle and my friends," he says.

We argue over what furniture to take with us. The list will be small. We're downsizing from a spacious Victorian home with a yard, gazebo, and garden to an apartment on the fourth floor of a converted warehouse in Cleveland. We will be getting rid of nearly everything we'd invested in over the last three years for our bed-and-breakfast. I think of what it will be like to listen to the country auctioneer taking lowball bids for the beds, the beautiful china, the rugs, the linens, the antique marble-topped dresser, and the vintage sideboard.

I feel like the prophet: "He has made me eat gravel, trampled me into the dust" (Lamentations 3:16, NABRE).

We're not just shedding material things. I'm losing a sense of myself as someone who can make something out of nothing, who can dream up opportunities and reinvent herself at will. My deepest nature is less pliable than I had thought. I'm not who I thought

I wanted to be. My husband is heartbroken, and I feel responsible. He liked my dream of being a country girl and an entrepreneur.

The prophet advises me to stop dwelling on the losses. It's the main reason my soul is deprived of peace. There's a list to be made of the opportunities too. They're there, if I'm honest. "To put one's mouth in the dust—there may yet be hope" (Lamentations 3:29, NABRE).

There is hope, along with the peace that always comes when I stop worrying and start trusting.

Let Us Pray

God, this experience is stripping me bare. May it make room in my life for more faith in You.

Further Reflection

2 CORINTHIANS 1:3–4 (NABRE)

Blessed be the God and Father of our Lord Jesus Christ, the Father of compassion and God of all encouragement, who encourages us in our every affliction, so that we may be able to encourage those who are in any affliction with the encouragement with which we ourselves are encouraged by God.

Reminders of Heaven

PATRICIA LORENZ

He will wipe away all tears from their eyes, and there shall be no more death, nor sorrow, nor crying, nor pain. All of that has gone forever.

REVELATION 21:4 (TLB)

Death slapped me in the face with a cold hand a few years ago. Between June and December, eight friends and neighbors and my husband's brother died.

In July, my dad, about to celebrate his ninety-fifth birthday, broke his back, causing some in our family to fear that the end was near.

In January, I was admitted to the hospital with what the doctors said was a life-threatening case of swine flu and a serious lung infection, forcing me to ponder the possibility of my own death. (After five days, I was discharged.)

The following April, Jeana, a vibrant fifty-two-year-old woman we'd had lunch with the first day of our European cruise, died suddenly in her cabin from diabetes and kidney complications. Death was on my mind every week during that stretch of time. One minute we're here enjoying life; the next minute we don't exist on this earth.

The only way I could reconcile the grief was to remind myself that, with the Lord, death equals heaven and heaven equals pure joy with God. The equation brought me peace, and I began to refocus on a life-centered equation. Life equals challenge and opportunity, and challenge and opportunity equal accomplishment and peace.

So there's really nothing to fear, either here on earth or in the afterlife. It's all good.

Let Us Pray

Heavenly Father, thank You for life here and in heaven. Bless all those I love and care about.

Further Reflection

1 CORINTHIANS 13:12–13 (TLB)

We can see and understand only a little about God now, as if we were peering at his reflection in a poor mirror; but someday we are going to see him in his completeness, face-to-face. Now all that I know is hazy and blurred, but then I will see everything clearly, just as clearly as God sees into my heart right now. There are three things that remain—faith, hope, and love—and the greatest of these is love.

Unexpected Peace

ERIN MacPHERSON

*Be still, and know that I am God.
I will be exalted among the nations,
I will be exalted in the earth!*

PSALM 46:10 (ESV)

It was one of those crazy, busy days.

My son had a poetry presentation right before my meeting with the principal about the PTA committee. Then I had to take my car to the shop to fix that scratch, and then go to swim practice, a soccer scrimmage, and church youth group. Somehow, in the midst of it all, I would have to figure out dinner and pick up a bottle of laundry detergent.

My mind began to race. *How was I going to get it all done?* I didn't have ten minutes to spare in my entire day. I grabbed my purse and my travel mug of coffee and hopped in the car, my heart beating fast, my adrenaline pumping.

I bit my lip and prayed. "Lord, I'm feeling so frantic. Please give me a little bit of peace today." Five minutes later, my prayer was answered. But not with a wave of indescribable peace, a little cheer-me-on pep talk from God, or a sense of calm in the midst of the chaos. Instead, God answered in the way I least expected.

My mom called: my grandmother had fallen and broken her hip. Surgery was scheduled. Instead of off to the school, I turned right toward the hospital. The scratch on the car could wait; swim practice, the scrimmage, and church youth group would have to be missed. Dinner would be in the hospital cafeteria. I would be spending my day in the quiet of a hospital room, holding my grandma's hand, reading Psalms, praying, singing, and being still.

Finding peace. Doing nothing but being exactly where I needed to be.

Let Us Pray

Father God, You answer prayers in the ways that we least expect. Yet, You always know precisely what we need. Help me to hear Your voice and be willing to respond to whatever it is You need me to do today.

Further Reflection

PSALM 62:12 (ESV)

And that to you, O Lord, belongs steadfast love. For you will render to a man according to his work.

Peace in the Pace

SABRA CIANCANELLI

*Be kind to one another, tenderhearted,
forgiving one another, as God in
Christ forgave you.*

EPHESIANS 4:32 (ESV)

I'd had an aching and restless heart all day. A family member casually said something hurtful, and I felt blindsided and attacked. I work with words all day, every day. I struggle to find the right ones, spend hours arranging and rearranging them, and so it seems I reexamined the hurtful words with an editor's eye. I analyzed the insult, turning it this way and that, searching for motivation, questioning word choice, and nitpicking the perceived offense. I deconstructed and reconstructed the affront a dozen times before I realized I was worsening the situation.

I called a friend and felt my anger rise as I went into great detail about what was said. I shooed away advice to simply let it go and found an excuse to hang up.

I turned to prayer but still rehashed the whole miserable, hurtful ordeal, complaining and complaining until I had worked myself up again.

When the restlessness didn't go away, I turned to cleaning. I scrubbed the kitchen cabinets and stove, and when that didn't help, I filled a pail with water, got on my hands and knees, and washed the floor.

The day was half over and my heart still felt tarnished. My mind raced with thoughts that were making me sick, so I put on my sneakers and went outside for a run. The air was cool. My pace quickened. Up one hill and down another, my breath grew fast and even. I lost myself in the pace. In the pace, I found peace. Right there, in that moment—my aching heart soared a little. I stopped in my tracks and took a deep, long, clearing breath, and a heaviness lifted, just enough for my heart to begin to mend.

Let Us Pray

Heavenly Father, forgiveness isn't easy. Guide me to heal my wounded heart, to stop focusing on things that hurt and instead lead me to Your comfort and love.

Further Reflection

JAMES 5:16 (ESV)

Therefore, confess your sins to one another and pray for one another, that you may be healed. The prayer of a righteous person has great power as it is working.

LUKE 6:27 (ESV)

"But I say to you who hear, Love your enemies, do good to those who hate you."

Growing with God

SHAWNELLE ELIASEN

The steadfast love of the LORD never ceases;
his mercies never come to an end.

LAMENTATIONS 3:22 (ESV)

It's the day our oldest son, Logan, graduates from law school. It's also the day we put an offer on a new home. Emotion is deep and wide.

My row of men sit and watch their brother receive his diploma. Logan stands, humble and strong, six foot one with a red beard. But I see my mop-headed little boy. The one I pushed on the swing while we sang. The one I read to. Built castles with from the edge of a sandbox. My mom understands and she squeezes my hand.

As Logan walks across the platform, pride and joy swell in my soul. We'd given him roots and wings, and this tension fills me. Watching our boy step into life, into who God made him to be, brings peace. But this is the final launch: He'll move away. We'll move into our new home.

Soon we're in a sea of celebration, searching for our son. When we finally see him, we rush over. The brothers cuff him on the back. Hug him tight. Logan scoops our youngest right off the floor. When a friend stops to congratulate Logan, Isaiah's feet go back to the ground.

Suddenly my dad is by my side. "Precious," he says. He nods toward my boys. "Logan's hand."

While Logan talks, he runs his fingers over the bristly softness of Isaiah's freshly cut hair. This simple, quiet tenderness runs rich with God's mercy. It flows through my family.

It's stronger than change.

It's mightier than letting go.

All of my sons will stretch and grow toward God's plan, and today Logan paves the way. The home we'll launch them from won't be the same one we brought them home to.

But I'm mindful of mercy, and all will be well.

Let Us Pray

Lord, Your mercy offers safety and strength.

Further Reflection

PSALM 116:5 (ESV)

Gracious is the LORD, and righteous; our God is merciful.

HEBREWS 4:16 (ESV)

Let us then with confidence draw near to the throne of grace, that we may receive mercy and find grace to help in time of need.

The Jesus Boat

CAROL KNAPP

He said to them, "Why are you afraid,
you men of little faith?" Then He got
up and rebuked the winds and the sea,
and it became perfectly calm.

MATTHEW 8:26 (NASB)

A spectacular story is told of Jesus in Matthew 8:23–27. He had been teaching large crowds and healing many who were ill. Then He and His disciples took their boat to the other side of the Sea of Galilee, a large freshwater lake.

Before they reached the opposite shore, a "great storm" swamped the boat with waves. This was an open wooden fishing boat, similar to the one exposed in 1986 when drought caused the Sea of Galilee waters to recede. One can presume Jesus was drenched and tossed about. His disciples—many of them seasoned fishermen—were terrified.

And Jesus? He was asleep. A deep, satisfying rest. The others had to wake Him, crying to Him to save them.

In the New American Standard Bible, the passage reads Jesus "rebuked the winds and the sea, and it became perfectly calm." He shut down the storm, imparting His peace to the forces of nature. His amazed disciples questioned, "What kind of a man is this, that even the winds and the sea obey Him?"

When I need to claim the peace of Jesus in a crisis, I climb in the "Jesus Boat"—what the ancient fishing vessel is frequently called. I found this deep, unexplainable rest in the storm most recently when I traveled the end-of-life journey with my beloved mother-in-law.

Mom's sudden illness broadsided us. Our family felt deluged by what was happening. I cried out to Jesus to speak His Word into Mom's life and for me to accept His authority. He invited me to trust Him, even as He welcomed Mom home with Him. His peace carried us across troubled waters.

Jesus can rebuke the storm, but to experience His calm in the storm is no less a miracle.

Let Us Pray

Son of God, in turbulent times, show me what it means to rest in—and with—You.

Further Reflection

EXODUS 33:14 (NASB)

And He said, "My presence shall go with you, and I will give you rest."

PSALM 62:1–2 (NASB)

My soul waits in silence for God alone; From Him comes my salvation. He alone is my rock and my salvation, My stronghold; I will not be greatly shaken.

Teamwork

ERIN MacPHERSON

His invisible attributes, namely, his eternal power and divine nature, have been clearly perceived, ever since the creation of the world, in the things that have been made.

ROMANS 1:20 (ESV)

It was a tense meeting, as meetings tend to be at select soccer tryouts.

We had just found out that certain teams were being divided, others were being formed, players were being moved, and coaches were being rearranged. People were upset and worried for their sons and daughters, and things began to get a bit more emotional than any of us had expected. Raised voices echoed across the fields. Angry feelings rose.

Then the coach stopped midsentence and pointed behind us. A brilliant orange full moon was rising over the tree line.

A collective gasp rippled through the crowd as the moon came fully into view. It's hard to describe that moment—the sunlight trickling away as streaks of moonlight burst into the sky. Every man, woman, and child standing there felt it. We were witnessing a moment of glory, a moment so beautiful and so inspiring that all else was momentarily forgotten.

We all stood there silently for a few minutes watching the sky light up. Lightning bugs floated around us as the moon rose and stars began to appear. Each of us seemed to breathe in the beauty and soak up the peace that came from what will be remembered as a magical moment.

I'm not sure if it was seconds or minutes later, but as if on cue, we all turned back to the coach and he began to speak again. Only now, the arguments and anger from before felt petty and insignificant. Worries about who would be on which soccer team, who would coach each team, and who would play which position suddenly felt silly.

It was soccer we were talking about. Youth soccer.

We had just witnessed the glory of God.

Let Us Pray

Jesus, when I start to worry about things that do not matter, pull my heart back to You.

Further Reflection

EXODUS 34:10 (ESV)

And he said, "Behold, I am making a covenant. Before all your people I will do marvels, such as have not been created in all the earth or in any nation. And all the people among whom you are shall see the work of the LORD, for it is an awesome thing that I will do with you."

Peace and Quiet

EVELYN BENCE

He leads me beside quiet waters,
he refreshes my soul.

PSALM 23:2–3 (NIV)

I've wondered why an adolescent neighbor friend has been eager to come to church with me for several months now. The service is traditional and liturgical. Think page-turning in hymnbooks and prayer books. Think stained-glass windows, a robed choir, and a somber doxology. It's not the jazzed-up hour that young teens stereotypically enjoy. It's not the exuberant Spanish church she attends when visiting her grandmother.

Last week, wondering if the novelty was wearing off, I asked, "Do you want to come again next week?"

"Definitely"—a word I'd never heard her use.

But a different phrase in her repertoire identifies her need that helps me understand the church's draw. Lately she's been asking for what she calls "peace and quiet" in her grandmother's kitchen or extended hours in my dining room. It's something she misses at home, where she shares a room with a rambunctious sister.

"Where did you hear about 'peace and quiet'?" I asked.

"It's what the teacher wants. Sometimes."

In chaotic seasons, I've sought out a serene setting, if not at church (some congregational worship services don't engender a beside-quiet-waters experience), then on a nature walk, at a courtyard fountain, or with soothing bedtime music.

In lonely times, when I've complained about having too much peace and quiet, I've allowed the Good Shepherd to fill and still my thirsty heart, soul, and mind—if not at church, then in a friend's kitchen or with an open book of psalms or songs.

Do I find refreshment?

Definitely. Eventually. God restores my soul.

Let Us Pray

Lord, lead me to a rippling brook or some other peaceful place where You can—and will—refresh my soul.

Further Reflection

ISAIAH 44:2–5 (NIV)

This is what the LORD says…"For I will pour water on the thirsty land, and streams on the dry ground; I will pour out my Spirit on your offspring, and my blessing on your descendants. They will spring up like grass in a meadow, like poplar trees by flowing streams. Some will say, 'I belong to the LORD'; others will call themselves by the name of Jacob; still others will write on their hand, 'The LORD's' and will take the name Israel."

Good to Go

AMY EDDINGS

Think of what is above, not of what is on earth. For you have died, and your life is hidden with Christ in God.

COLOSSIANS 3:2–3 (NABRE)

Friends and acquaintances ask me how I'm doing, weeks now after my father has died. "I'm doing really well," I tell them. "His death was amazing."

My dad got very sick, very suddenly. He died of multiple organ failure two days after going to the hospital complaining of severe abdominal pain.

We were all with him when he died—Mom and my five siblings. We took turns witnessing the joy he gave us and the meaning his life held for us.

"Dad," I said, holding his face between my hands, "are you ready? Are you good to go?"

His words were barely a whisper: "I'm fine."

I needed to know if he was scared. He let me know that he wasn't. I could let him go.

I had no unresolved issues with my father. I have no feelings of "if only," no doubts about his love for me or whether I had made him proud. He told me so, told my siblings, all the time, bucking the parenting tendencies of the men of his generation. He was affectionate and generous with praise and encouragement. He was never rude or impolite, mocking or mean, and so we had no need to seek resolution or reconciliation. He was, indeed, good to go.

We put our hands on him. His breaths came in short sips, and then they stopped coming altogether. I had the curious feeling of being a spectator at the finish line of a long and spirited race. I thought of Dad like a runner, leaning in to break the tape, the bonds of earth, the veil between here and the "what's next." A deep peace and quiet joy settled over us. It is with me still.

Let Us Pray

God, show me how to lead a good life so that
I may experience a good death. Help me to be
good to go when it's my time.

Further Reflection

REVELATION 21:4 (NABRE)

He will wipe every tear from their eyes, and there shall be no more death or mourning, wailing or pain, [for] the old order has passed away.

REVELATION 22:4–5 (NABRE)

They will look upon his face, and his name will be on their foreheads. Night will be no more, nor will they need light from lamp or sun, for the Lord God shall give them light, and they shall reign forever and ever.

Soul Remodel

BILL GIOVANNETTI

I pray that out of his glorious riches he may strengthen you with power through his Spirit in your inner being, so that Christ may dwell in your hearts through faith.

EPHESIANS 3:16–17 (NIV)

It was a double whammy. A major move and a major remodel. We tore up our new house before we moved in. We ripped out floors, gutted the kitchen, tore up two bathrooms, and then moved in right in the middle of the chaos.

The next three months saw a steady stream of workers invading our sanctuary. They pounded and painted and sawed. My family dodged tools and debris. Boxes sat unopened, piled high in the garage. Furniture waited for flooring. Boxes waited for furniture. Our only stove was the grill outside. Our only refrigerator was an old clunker in the garage. Fast food became a reluctant blessing. Chaos reigned.

We endured paint fumes, early-morning hammering, daily disruption, dust, displacement, and disorder. My wife selected light fixtures and countertops. We built new walls, installed new floors, and constructed an essentially new house.

All of this to take somebody else's plan and transform it into a home that reflected our style, our personality, and our plan.

During the middle of the mess, I drove home one day and sat in the driveway. Contractors' pickup trucks flanked me. I was tired of the chaos. As I lingered in the quiet car, I felt God's whisper. "Your heart is My home. I'm using these stresses to create in you something beautiful. One that reflects My style. My grace. My plan."

Peace flooded in. God was doing in me what we were doing in our house. The results in our home were spectacular. My wife's tasteful eye turned a house I dreaded into a home I love. I hope God says the same about the dwelling place He's crafting in my soul.

Let Us Pray

Lord, make my heart a dwelling place where You truly feel at home.

Further Reflection

MATTHEW 7:24–25 (NIV)

Therefore everyone who hears these words of mine and puts them into practice is like a wise man who built his house on the rock. The rain came down, the streams rose, and the winds blew and beat against that house; yet it did not fall, because it had its foundation on the rock.

2 TIMOTHY 2:15, 21 (NIV)

Do your best to present yourself to God as one approved, a worker who does not need to be ashamed and who correctly handles the word of truth. . . . Those who cleanse themselves from the latter will be instruments for special purposes, made holy, useful to the Master and prepared to do any good work.

Content in the Cold

ERIKA BENTSEN

*I have learned to be content
whatever the circumstances.*

PHILIPPIANS 4:11 (NIV)

The Apostle Paul's encouragement to be content whatever the circumstances was my devotional lesson for the day. I grimace at the thermometer. Minus 10 degrees? This is going to be hard. My breath puffs into clouds as I trudge through the snow with a larger-than-usual armload of hay for my horse. Jack thrusts his frosty muzzle into the hay. At least *he* looks content. I grab the ax to chop ice on the water trough. A few whacks and I open a small hole in the ice. One hearty swing to widen the hole and—*ping! Splash!* The spacer holding the ax together shoots off into the hole. I reach for the ax head, but it's too late. It scuds harmlessly along the bottom of the trough, but I'm not sticking my arm in three feet of ice water to retrieve it.

Wanting to lower the power bill, I'd put the electric tank heater away the week before during an unseasonable warm-up.

It had been easy to be content then. I shake my wet glove. Contentment in this? Impossible! *Why, God?* I break trail to the pump house and kick snow away from the door just enough to reach the tank heater on the shelf. *Why is the pump running? Is that water dripping?* The pressure valve is broken; water pours from the tank. I stretch from the door jamb to shut off the power to the well. At least it's a cement building. Standing water would have destroyed wood.

I kneel in inches of water to remove the broken valve. I laugh suddenly when it hits me. *That's why, God.* Content with minus 10 degrees? I'm rejoicing in it instead! Praise God for minus 10 degrees, and praise God for the broken ax—otherwise I wouldn't have opened the pump-house door until June!

Let Us Pray

Praise You, Lord, for broken things that guide
us toward unexpected blessings. Yes, in this
we can be more than content.

Further Reflection

ROMANS 12:12 (NIV)

Be joyful in hope, patient in affliction, faithful in prayer.

1 CORINTHIANS 13:7 (NIV)

It always protects, always trusts, always hopes, always perseveres.

Sailing through Peace

JULIA ATTAWAY

The Spirit of God was hovering over the face of the waters.

GENESIS 1:2 (ESV)

Pier 66 was filled with chattering teens and parents and sailing instructors for the "Back to the River" celebration of my son's after-school program. The sun was shining and the waters of the Hudson gleaming. It was the initiation of the spring season when students launched the small craft they'd built during the long winter months.

The good news was that no one's boat sank. The better news was that each Monday from now on the youngsters would be sailing again. Putting teens in boats isn't what people normally think of when they imagine what public school in New York City is like. But my Manhattan-born and -bred fourteen-year-old, who used to be familiar only with navigating crowded subways, has taken to the water with surprising ease.

He arrives home exhausted each Monday after maneuvering around cruise ships, through tides, and in the wake of speedboats. His sailing friends are almost all from different countries, neighborhoods, and ethnic backgrounds. The river—and a nonprofit called Hudson River Community Sailing—bring them together.

I chose an empanada from the potluck table and steered myself and my cup of lemonade toward a bench at the end of the pier. This was Stephen's territory, not mine. I wondered if

I was supposed to talk to people and decided that for today it was fine to let someone else take the initiative. I would rest in the sunshine, enjoy my spicy meal, and observe my son. He and his buddies clustered nearby, chatting in their newly deep voices and eating vast quantities of pizza.

Periodically Stephen glanced my way as if to say, *I'm glad you are here, even if I'm hanging out with my friends.* That was enough. I was near the water, near my son, and a light wind blew in contentment like the breath of the Spirit. What more could I ask?

Let Us Pray

**Holy Spirit, move over my heart
and stir up love within it.**

Further Reflection

DEUTERONOMY 6:5–9 (ESV)

You shall love the LORD your God with all your heart and with all your soul and with all your might. And these words that I command you today shall be on your heart. You shall teach them diligently to your children, and shall talk of them when you sit in your house, and when you walk by the way, and when you lie down, and when you rise. You shall bind them as a sign on your hand, and they shall be as frontlets between your eyes. You shall write them on the doorposts of your house and on your gates.

Rest for a Weary Soul

SCOTT WALKER

I call to you, LORD, every day;
I spread out my hands to you.

PSALM 88:9 (NIV)

This morning, I quietly entered my office and sank down in my old easy chair. I did not turn on the lights. I wanted to fade into the shadows, close my eyes, and be silent. I was tired. Eight good hours of sleep each night evades me. And the pace of life does not slow down. In the midst of many people, I often grow lonely.

After a moment of stillness, my lips moved and I subliminally intoned the words of a hymn by Charles Wesley: "Father, I stretch my hands to Thee, no other help I know; If Thou withdraw Thyself from me, Ah! whither shall I go?"

What I need most from God is the realization of His presence with me. And what God needs most from me is my desire to live in close relationship with Him. I love theology and Bible study and rich devotional literature. But I yearn most for an intuitive awareness of God within me. John Wesley, the charismatic founder of the Methodist church, prayed for this same presence. And Jesus did too.

There is a rest that only God can bring to a weary soul. And there is a joy that warms the heart of God when we lift our hands and spirits toward Him.

Let Us Pray

**Father, I stretch my hands to You.
There is no other help I need. Amen.**

Further Reflection

PSALM 42:1–2, 7–8 (NIV)

As the deer pants for streams of water, so my soul pants for you, my God. My soul thirsts for God, for the living God. When can I go and meet with God?...Deep calls to deep in the roar of your waterfalls; all your waves and breakers have swept over me. By day the Lord directs his love, at night his song is with me—a prayer to the God of my life.

JAMES 4:8 (NIV)

Come near to God and he will come near to you. Wash your hands, you sinners, and purify your hearts, you double-minded.

Change of Plans

LOGAN ELIASEN

I have said these things to you, that in me you may have peace. In the world you will have tribulation. But take heart; I have overcome the world.

JOHN 16:33 (ESV)

I have a thousand things to do: reading assignments, notes to review, a spin class in an hour. I walk down the path that runs from the law school to the parking lot. I'm wearing headphones, listening to an audio recording of a lecture. I hate how rushed I am, but this is the life stage I'm in right now. Next month, I'll graduate; I'm hoping that things will slow down.

I look up and see a ceiling of thin, new leaves covering the path. A week ago, the trees were just budding. In the intervening days of gray and rain, the leaves had surreptitiously unfolded.

I reach the edge of the parking lot, and my eyes are drawn to two trees. They are ten feet apart, straight and strong. In the past, I used them to hang my portable hammock. I wish I had time to do that now, but I have to keep moving.

When I reach my car, I swing my backpack off my shoulder and into the trunk. I open the driver's door, then look at my watch: fifteen minutes to spare. So instead of sliding into the seat, I reach under it and pull out a tightly wrapped bundle. My hammock is right where I left it last fall.

I return to the twin oaks and wrap a strap around each one. Then I clip my hammock into place and wriggle into a cocoon of parachute fabric.

The hammock sways back and forth. I take off my headphones and listen to the branches creaking in the breeze. I still have a list of things to do, and, in a moment, I will return to it.

But today there is sunshine. And I would be a fool to let the day slip by without soaking up just a few minutes of the beauty and rest that God provided.

Let Us Pray

Father, thank You for giving us sunshine and reprieve.

Further Reflection

PSALM 23:1–3 (NIV)

The LORD is my shepherd, I lack nothing. He makes me lie down in green pastures, he leads me beside quiet waters, he refreshes my soul. He guides me along the right paths for his name's sake.

MARK 6:31 (NIV)

Then, because so many people were coming and going that they did not even have a chance to eat, he said to them, "Come with me by yourselves to a quiet place and get some rest."

Take a Walk

MARILYN TURK

*If I rise on the wings of the dawn, if
I settle on the far side of the sea, even
there your hand will guide me, your
right hand will hold me fast.*

PSALM 139:9–10 (NIV)

I wanted to run away. Life was getting out of control. The burdens were weighing me down.

Texts and calls to a son who lived out of state went unanswered. My imagination went to the worst-possible scenarios. Is he in trouble? Sick? Hurt?

Another son was upset about a relationship gone bad.

And we had our grandson, Logan, to care for. The day-to-day challenges of raising a young child wore on my husband and me. I couldn't share my distress with my husband, though, because he was having his own issues with our situation. There really wasn't anyone I could talk to, except God. But I wondered if He remembered me, since my prayers seemed to be going unanswered.

I couldn't run away from my problems, so I opted for a walk instead—someplace I hadn't been before, a place where I wouldn't see any neighbors who required conversation. I took off away from my home and walked past familiar streets, not knowing where I was going. After I'd walked some distance, I turned down a street I hadn't been on before and headed

toward the bay that surrounds the area. Seeing a vacant lot, I crossed it to the shore, where I found remnants of an old pier. I sat by the water and talked to God. Soon the tears flowed. Was God listening? Did He even know I still exist?

The water's gentle, rhythmic lapping on the small beach calmed me, and peace washed over me. I lifted my eyes to the sky and heard the reassuring words of God in Psalm 139:9–10. He did remember me.

Let Us Pray

Dear Father, thank You for not forgetting me and for caring about my concerns.

Further Reflection

ISAIAH 41:10 (NIV)

So do not fear, for I am with you; do not be dismayed, for I am your God. I will strengthen you and help you; I will uphold you with my righteous right hand.

DEUTERONOMY 31:6 (NIV)

Be strong and courageous. Do not be afraid or terrified because of them, for the LORD your God goes with you; he will never leave you nor forsake you.

Beach Prayer

PATRICIA LORENZ

Let everyone bless God and sing his praises;
for he holds our lives in his hands,
and he holds our feet to the path.

PSALM 66:8–9 (TLB)

I always wondered why my prayer life perks up when I'm at the beach; sometimes I find it easier to pray there than at church. My beach on the Gulf of Mexico is near my home, just a mile and a half away. When I'm there for four hours, I am in the water for three. The rest of the time, I'm walking barefoot in the warm sand looking for interesting shells, chatting with other beachgoers, or saying my prayers.

One day, I read about a study providing evidence that the beach is the best place to recharge and unwind because it promotes good health, physically and mentally. Sea air is charged with negative ions that produce antidepressant effects and help balance serotonin levels, which help greatly with seasonal affective disorder. The repetitive sound of the waves crashing on the shore can calm your mind. Even the blue color of the water is psychologically soothing. The high levels of magnesium, potassium, and iodine, the minerals in sea water, help fight infection, heal the body of minor cuts and scrapes, and detoxify. Walking barefoot in the sand strengthens foot muscles too.

I cherish all those benefits of going to the beach, but the one I like the most is how easy the prayers come when I'm totally relaxed and floating in salt water. Every time I'm at the beach, whether I'm swimming, snorkeling, jumping the waves, floating, or kicking around, I'm in such a relaxed state that meditation, prayer, and counting my blessings just come naturally. You may not have easy access to a beach, but God wants to meet you wherever you pray.

Let Us Pray

Heavenly Father, maker of the oceans, lakes, rivers, and seas, keep giving me the grace to use my beach time as prayer time. Thank You for such a perfect outdoor cathedral.

Further Reflection

PSALM 107:29 (TLB)

He calms the storm and stills the waves.

JEREMIAH 29:12 (TLB)

In those days when you pray, I will listen.

COLOSSIANS 4:2 (TLB)

Don't be weary in prayer; keep at it; watch for God's answers, and remember to be thankful when they come.

Give Up the Fight

ASHLEY KAPPEL

The LORD will fight for you;
you need only to be still.

EXODUS 14:14 (NIV)

L ook out!" my son James cried, imaginary sword in hand. It didn't matter that I was trying to cook dinner; there was obviously a shark trying to devour me, and James was my shining knight.

I played along, crying out for help, tippy-tapping my feet while I chopped veggies, until James appeared to lose interest. While he had been backstroking on my kitchen hardwoods to reach the beast, he suddenly stood up and walked away.

"Where are you going?" I asked. "I thought you were going to save me from this shark!"

He shrugged. "Only God can save you now, Mommy."

I used to doubt people when they told me things their children had said. Then I had James. James learned to talk in full sentences at eighteen months because it was about time someone understood him. He changed his name when he was barely two, telling me Jake, the nickname we'd always intended to call him, "is a baby name. I'm James now." At three, he can repeat movies verbatim, which is great, until he's in line at a birthday party and yells, "Olivia! I'm tired of looking at your [you-know-what]!" (Thanks, Ferdinand.)

But I have always believed that James has a wise, old soul. He feels things deeply and responds passionately. The day he gave up saving me from the shark must've been hard on his hero heart, but it showed me that even a three-year-old can know when it's time to fully lean on God to help finish off those pesky sharks.

If you're facing a shark in your life, rest easy. God is here fighting for you, and He has way more than an imaginary sword.

Let Us Pray

Lord, save me from the sharks nipping at my heels today. Help me remember that I can give up the fight and fully lean on You in times of trial.

Further Reflection

DEUTERONOMY 3:22 (NIV)

Do not be afraid of them; the LORD your God himself will fight for you.

2 CHRONICLES 20:17 (NIV)

You will not have to fight this battle. Take up your positions; stand firm and see the deliverance the LORD will give you, Judah and Jerusalem. Do not be afraid; do not be discouraged. Go out to face them tomorrow, and the LORD will be with you.

EPHESIANS 2:8–9 (NIV)

For it is by grace you have been saved, through faith—and this is not from yourselves, it is the gift of God—not by works, so that no one can boast.

A Nourishing View

EVELYN BENCE

May the favor of the Lord our God rest on us; establish the work of our hands for us.

PSALM 90:17 (NIV)

At lunchtime, I usually throw together a sandwich. I eat it in my home office, in front of my computer with a view of swaying oak branches outside the window. But my workload is light this week. This noon, I changed my venue. With plate and cup, I settled into a living room chair. Nagging questions quickly surfaced: *Should I be pushing to generate new projects? Or stepping back to catch my breath?* In the respite, my eyes rested on a tableau of framed prints that defines the interior wall across the room.

I started collecting the pieces decades ago for my first apartment when I clipped a tinted photo from a perfume ad. Then at a yard sale, I found an Andrew Wyeth—an inviting empty chair beside a window. My mom gave me her heirloom copy of Millet's *The Gleaners*, still in its vintage frame. I later added prints bought at museum shops: a Vermeer *Girl with the Red*

Hat, a Sargent mother and daughter, a Morisot, and more—twelve in all.

It had been too long since I'd spent time with the personalized gallery. This noon's vantage point reminded me that in this apartment I'd grouped the scenes by universal themes. Those on the right depict labor: subjects ironing laundry, peeling onions, harvesting fields. Those on the left strike a meditative pose: serene portraits, dreamy lovers, inspired musicians.

A few moments with the art settled my spirit. In the array, I saw the interplaying modes of life, even of a particular day. *It's not all demanding work. It's not all rest or reflection. Why not make room for both?*

I plan to eat tomorrow's sandwich away from my desk, maybe outside under the oak. The sandwich will nourish my body. A new vista might nourish and replenish my soul.

Let Us Pray

Lord, help me to find a good balance
between work and rest.

Further Reflection

ECCLESIASTES 3:1 (NIV)

There is a time for everything, and a season for every activity under the heavens.

ISAIAH 30:18 (NIV)

The LORD longs to be gracious to you; therefore he will rise up to show you compassion. For the LORD is a God of justice. Blessed are all who wait for him!

The Prayer Chain

ERIKA BENTSEN

*For You are with me; Your rod
and Your staff, they comfort me.*

PSALM 23:4 (NKJV)

I winced when the chiropractor put his finger on my spine. "I can't fix this. The vertebrae are fine. This is a disk issue. You need surgery."

No, God! Not again! I limped to my pickup. I was never going to have another surgery, not after the first operation for a ruptured disk four years ago had failed. I'd given up the life I loved as a cattle rancher. *I have nothing left, God. You have taken everything away from me.*

I texted my brother: "Pray 4 me. I need strength."

He replied immediately. "Will do."

I called my husband. "Maybe this is a blessing in disguise," he said. "Your back hasn't been right for years. Maybe this time you'll be healed."

I didn't share his optimism. I'd already tried Western medicine, Eastern medicine, and everything in between. I tried different doctors, no doctors, and doctors I wasn't too sure about. I did natural cures, yoga, vitamins, joint solutions, tilt tables, back exercises, brain exercises, and meditation.

Some things helped a little, but nothing really worked. I had long ago accepted my limitations. I'd even found joy here. But this new explosion of pain left me without hope.

Suddenly, unexpected peace stopped my tears. Confused, I glanced at my phone, which I'd silenced. "You're on the prayer chain at church," my brother texted.

I could feel the prayers. The one thing that had gotten me through these painful years was my faith that God was behind this and was guiding me to a new place of His choosing. He was with me. I wasn't alone.

Let Us Pray

Lord, I'm closer to You now than ever before.
Even if I never heal, I would rather be crippled
with You than stand tall without You.

Further Reflection

GENESIS 26:24 (NKJV)

And the LORD appeared to him the same night and said, "I am the God of your father Abraham; do not fear, for I am with you. I will bless you and multiply your descendants for My servant Abraham's sake."

DEUTERONOMY 31:6 (NKJV)

Be strong and of good courage, do not fear nor be afraid of them; for the LORD your God, He is the One who goes with you. He will not leave you nor forsake you.

Right Where I'm Meant to Be

BUCK STORM

*But wanting to justify himself, he said
to Jesus, "And who is my neighbor?"*

LUKE 10:29 (NASB)

*B*roke *and broken down.*

The words kept running through my mind. After three weeks of ministry concert dates and a couple of thousand miles under our wheels, my family and I were finally pointed toward home when our old motorhome decided enough was enough. Now we were stuck in a junkyard garage on the edge of a windswept plain in the middle of nowhere. I wasn't sure I could even afford the tow, let alone labor and parts.

God and I thumb-wrestled, and my bitterness edged out. *Lord, why now? Why here?*

Desperate to hurry things along, I looked down at the elderly mechanic. "Hey, man, is there anything I can do to help?"

He blinked at me through thick glasses. "Actually, yeah. Can you grab a half-inch wrench out of the toolbox and hold that bolt right there?"

A few minutes later, I was covered in grease to my elbows.

An hour after that, I realized that the man on the other side of the engine wasn't just an oil-smeared face. His name was Bob. He'd lost the wife of his youth to cancer. Recently

he'd come out of retirement to make the extra cash he needed to raise his two grandsons.

Why here? Why now? Simple—because God loved Bob.

As we talked on through the hours, I realized that I loved Bob too. My bitterness had tumbled off over the grass with the prairie wind.

Later, I held my breath as the shop owner totaled the bill.

Then he smiled. "You know what? I'm only gonna charge you for parts. The rest is on me. Bob really needed someone to talk to."

I left humbled. Bob and I had worn the grease, but the Great Mechanic had done the work.

Let Us Pray

**Lord, help me to see past myself
so that I might see You.**

Further Reflection

ISAIAH 1:17 (NASB)

Learn to do good; Seek justice, Rebuke the oppressor, Obtain justice for the orphan, Plead for the widow's case.

JOHN 13:34 (NASB)

I am giving you a new commandment, that you love one another; just as I have loved you, that you also love one another.

A Hopeful Future

CARLA HENDRICKS

There is neither Jew nor Gentile, neither slave nor free, nor is there male and female, for you are all one in Christ Jesus.

GALATIANS 3:28 (NIV)

Recently, my husband began co-leading community discussions on racial unity in our growing city in Tennessee. At the end of one of these discussions, my husband's co-leader invited audience members to share their personal experiences with race.

After listening to a few others' testimonies, I rose from my seat and walked to the podium. Accompanied by my thumping heartbeat and shaking hands, I shared my family's story as minorities in a largely homogeneous city. I spoke of vandalism at my son's middle school, with racially offensive words written on a wall in the boys' bathroom. I shared the day my husband and I discovered similarly offensive words painted on utility boxes on our lawn in a neighborhood where we were the only African American family. I recounted the fear that gripped me the night a police officer pulled over my college-age son as I drove nearby, praying he would remember the safety protocol my husband and I had taught him.

As I shared story after story, I felt empathy from others in the room. I saw tears pool in the eyes of a few. When I walked away from the podium, I was encouraged that our community had begun this conversation on race that would continue through future challenges we might face. I was hopeful that now we could face them together.

Near the end of his "I Have a Dream" speech, Dr. Martin Luther King Jr. proclaimed these words, "Let freedom ring from Lookout Mountain of Tennessee." I believe Dr. King would be proud of this small community in Tennessee, filled with people of different races and cultures sharing, listening, and lamenting with one another.

Let Us Pray

Lord may we, Your children, continue to fight
for unity, peace, and love.

Further Reflection

1 SAMUEL 16:7 (NIV)

But the LORD said to Samuel, "Do not consider his appearance or his height, for I have rejected him. The LORD does not look at the things people look at. People look at the outward appearance, but the LORD looks at the heart."

1 CORINTHIANS 12:13 (NIV)

For we were all baptized by one Spirit so as to form one body—whether Jews or Gentiles, slave or free—and we were all given the one Spirit to drink.

Baiting for Happiness

BROCK KIDD

Happy is the man . . . that getteth understanding.

PROVERBS 3:13 (KJV)

I send my favorite fly sailing across the surface of the water. *Plop.* It lands in the exact spot that I had targeted. The pure joy I felt as a small child, sitting on the pier beside my dad, surrounds me. The pressures of work and the anxiety of the world fall away. Here, at the water's edge, I am content.

The ways to catch a fish are just as varied as the people who pursue the sport. There are bait fishermen, who use live bait like minnows and worms. They take a bare hook tied under a float or bobber, bait the hook, and then throw it out into the water and sit patiently until it bobs up and down. Then there are lure fishermen, who use different types of buzz baits, plugs, and spinners—and there are hundreds of colors, types, and styles. Finally, my favorite, fly fishing. From studying the local habitat to choosing a fly that most represents the insects currently hatching on the river, it's like becoming one with the spot where I've chosen to fish.

Fishing is all about "catching the big one." Catching happiness is much the same.

We all cast about in our own ways to find peace, happiness, and, ultimately, God. Like fishing, each person has his or her own style. Some of us crave action; others want the quiet satisfaction that comes with sitting on the shore. But aren't we all looking for that perfect spot where we become one with our Father God?

Successful fishing takes a lot of effort. I'm resolved to try even harder to search for and find the peace that God offers. On a grassy bank, by a quiet stream, in a boat on a calm lake, by the mighty ocean's edge, I know He's there, waiting for each of us, hoping we catch the happiness that He offers.

Let Us Pray

Father, Your presence is my finest catch.

Further Reflection

PSALM 35:9 (KJV)

And my soul shall be joyful in the LORD: it shall rejoice in his salvation.

PROVERBS 19:8 (KJV)

He that getteth wisdom loveth his own soul: he that keepeth understanding shall find good.

ECCLESIASTES 2:26 (KJV)

For God giveth to a man that is good in his sight wisdom, and knowledge, and joy: but to the sinner he giveth travail, to gather and to heap up, that he may give to him that is good before God. This also is vanity and vexation of spirit.

Be Present

ASHLEY KAPPEL

*Do not worry, saying, "What shall
we eat?" or "What shall we drink?"
or "What shall we wear?"*

MATTHEW 6:31 (NIV)

Each year, my family (thirty-one and counting!) heads to the beach to run relay races on the shore, have Bible lessons with Nana, play for hours in the pool, and eat family style for twenty-one meals straight.

When our five-year-old daughter, Olivia, looked at the calendar and saw that the beach was still *pages* away, she sighed, "It'll never get here!" with the dramatic despair that only a five-year-old can conjure. I offered her the chance to skip ahead.

"We could go to the beach right now," I told her. Her eyes lit up! "But your cousins can't come this week, so they won't be there. And you'll miss Vacation Bible School. And your dance recital, Charlotte's birthday, and your school field trip." Her eyes narrowed.

"Do you want to skip all those things?" I asked her, in a neutral tone.

"No!" she said, aghast I'd even make such an offer.

With that, we chose a family motto: "Be present." The Bible tells us not to be anxious, but in my child's case, she was anxious to get this party going! So this year, we're being present.

We work on this daily. Rushing through dinner won't get you a treat any faster. Wishing away a school week won't make the weekend come sooner. Trying to fast-forward rest time only means you'll be tired when we ride bikes this evening. Instead, be present, which is really the only place you can be anyway, and find joy where you are.

Let Us Pray

Lord, thank You for the reminder to slow way
down and drink in the beauty of each day.

Further Reflection

HEBREWS 13:5 (NIV)

Keep your lives free from the love of money and be content with what you have, because God has said, "Never will I leave you; never will I forsake you."

1 PETER 5:7 (NIV)

Cast all your anxiety on him because he cares for you.

Walking in Christ

GAYLE T. WILLIAMS

A friend loves at all times, and a brother is born for a time of adversity.

PROVERBS 17:17 (NIV)

Since I began my adult walk with Christ, I became keenly aware of people and their actions. I began to notice that there were people placed in my path who showed me God's love and light, wherever I went.

My forever friend David always relied heavily upon his faith to get through the challenges of high school and college. While I wallowed in my worries, David moved through similar concerns with a confidence I couldn't understand. But I knew he prayed regularly and went to Mass diligently. There was something different about David. I suspect it was the Christ in him.

A coworker, Jackie, who was solidly walking along with God in her life, once asked why I didn't go to church regularly. To her, it was a simple question. To me, it was a turning point. I didn't have a reason for not attending church, except that I hadn't yet found one that I wanted to join.

After caring for twenty toddlers all day, Andrea, my son's preschool teacher, spent her evenings caring for her elderly and infirm parents. Nevertheless, she came to work, lovingly cared for children, sang them to sleep, and kept them smiling, even when they missed their mommies. I visited Andrea once at her home, observed her caring for her parents, and saw all her love. I love the Christ in her.

Each of these friends offered me clear proof about how putting God first and relying upon Him can propel you through life's challenges. When I saw the Christ in Andrea, Jackie, and David, I knew I wanted that peace in my own life.

Let Us Pray

Heavenly Father, thank You for the people who
follow You, whom You so strategically place in
our lives to offer us tangible examples of
how to be better disciples.

Further Reflection

PSALM 125:4 (NIV)

LORD, do good to those who are good, to those who are upright in heart.

EZEKIEL 20:19 (NIV)

I am the LORD your God; follow my decrees and be careful to keep my laws.

Just a Few Moments

SHAWNELLE ELIASEN

*But seek first the kingdom of God
and his righteousness, and all
these things will be added to you.*

MATTHEW 6:33 (ESV)

A storm brought us together.

Lonny and I huddled in the living room with our sons. The power was out, and the younger boys were restless. Their flashlights threw beams of light.

"Let's make shadow animals," one boy said. That lasted ten minutes.

"I know," another son said. "Let's sing 'Row, Row, Row Your Boat' in a round." He started singing, and the brothers joined in. Lonny and I came in at the end, and our choruses melded together every time.

"See," my husband whispered, "we can't stay apart. We meet even in a song."

I pressed into his arms, on our old sofa, in our home filled to the brim with boys. Just a few moments together made me understand that we'd been missing out.

It can be the same with God. I have every intention of beginning each day with Him. I have a special chair. My Bible is page-marked. But sometimes I hit the snooze button. Or I wake and want to tackle dirty dishes from the night before.

It's when I go back that I understand how I've missed God. His Word becomes the heartbeat that draws me in, and I'm content and filled, settled and stilled. Focused time in His presence is the sustaining grace I need.

Lonny's arms stayed strong around me, and we waited out the storm. One of our sons found a favorite book and read out loud. I tried, but I couldn't follow. I was lost in thoughts of God's love.

Let Us Pray

Lord, may time alone with You be something I can't do without. Amen.

Further Reflection

PSALM 5:3 (ESV)

O LORD, in the morning you hear my voice; in the morning I prepare a sacrifice for you and watch.

PSALM 119:47 (ESV)

For I find my delight in your commandments, which I love.

MARK 1:35 (ESV)

And rising very early in the morning, while it was still dark, he departed and went out to a desolate place, and there he prayed.

With Me Always

ERIN JANOSO

He spreads the snow like wool and
scatters the frost like ashes.

PSALM 147:16 (NIV)

I stared out the window at an opaque gray sky. The very late-season snow was falling fast. Just yesterday, my young daughter and I were delighting over the green chives she'd spotted pushing up through the brown mud. What welcome harbingers of the long-awaited spring!

But now everything was frozen under another deep layer of winter. The scene felt as bleak as my mood. The night before, my husband and I had quarreled bitterly. Old wounds reared their ugly heads, and weaponized words like "you never" and "you're always" flew. We both knew better and were past stooping to those lows. Or so I'd thought.

Turns out I'd been silly to think spring had finally arrived. And I'd been a fool to think we would ever rise above our flaws.

Donning my jacket, I stepped out onto the deck. The cold bit at my cheeks as I looked up at the tall spruce trees surrounding the cabin. It was so quiet I could hear the whispers the snowflakes made as they hit the ground.

Slowly, a peace enveloped me, quieting my churning mind. I made my way over to where we'd found the chives and pushed the snow aside. There they were, as bright and green and full of life as they'd been the day before. They'd been protected from the bitter cold by the same layer of fluffy white snow I'd been so upset about.

As I turned to go back inside, my heart felt lighter. Maybe last night's quarrel wasn't as grim as it had seemed either. After all, my husband and I, and our marriage, were covered by a protective blanket of our own: God's love. With Him in our corner, we could weather any storm.

Let Us Pray

The protections You provide come in so many different forms. Thank You, God, for the reminder that Your love is with me always.

Further Reflection

PSALM 121:1-4 (NIV)

I lift up my eyes to the mountains—where does my help come from? My help comes from the LORD, the Maker of heaven and earth. He will not let your foot slip—he who watches over you will not slumber.

ROMANS 8:31 (NIV)

What, then, shall we say in response to these things? If God is for us, who can be against us?

Ordinary Moments, Extraordinary Results

CAROL KUYKENDALL

God is our refuge and strength,
A very present help in trouble.

PSALM 46:1 (NKJV)

I have trouble falling asleep sometimes, probably because in the quiet darkness, I often start thinking about troubling things. Recently, I started doing something different that's helping.

No spiritual rocket science here. I just practice *gratitude*, in bed, in the dark.

Here's my routine: I usually read a little before turning out the light and snuggling under the comforter. (I love that it's called a "comforter.") Then I begin a quick review of the goodness that surrounds me at that moment and in my day that is ending.

Last night, my first thankful thought was for my husband, who was peacefully asleep next to me. Then I thanked God for the feel and smell of the clean sheets I put on our bed that day.

Next, I remembered a moment in church that morning when I looked around and saw so many people I know and feel known by. I know their stories; they know mine, which brings such comfort. I also saw people I didn't yet know whose stories will stretch me and bring new life into our community.

Finally, I thought of the fresh, ripe red strawberries in our refrigerator. They are in season now, and I love how they look and how they tasted today.

These are ordinary things and ordinary moments that might easily be taken for granted, but they become sacred and comforting when I recognize God's presence in all that is good. I thank Him, which is a good way to end the day.

Then I fall asleep filled with gratitude rather than worries.

Let Us Pray

Lord, acknowledging You as the faithful Giver of all goodness in my days helps me sleep peacefully.

Further Reflection

GENESIS 28:16 (NKJV)

Then Jacob awoke from his sleep and said, "Surely the LORD is in this place, and I did not know it."

Never Lost

BILL GIOVANNETTI

For I am persuaded that neither death nor life, nor angels nor principalities nor powers, nor things present nor things to come, nor height nor depth, nor any other created thing, shall be able to separate us from the love of God which is in Christ Jesus our Lord.

ROMANS 8:38–39 (NKJV)

Our family had spent an afternoon at the movies, watching the latest installment of a nostalgic cartoon from my kids' childhood. On the way out, my daughter, Josie, realized she had lost her sunglasses.

After a quick search of the theater, we found nothing. My son and I volunteered to see if she had left them in the car. Sure enough, they were in the backseat, and soon we were headed home. With one child in college and one almost in college, it was a rare treat to have our whole family together.

Josie turned the conversation spiritual. "What if I lost God?" she said. "Or what if God lost me?" We quickly realized she wasn't joking. With a tender conscience and a spiritually attuned heart, her sense of security with God had been a long-running question mark.

Margi asked, "Josie, do you actually think you're like God's sunglasses and He's forgetful like you, so He forgot where He put you?"

She laughed and shook her head. "No, but what if it happened?"

Her younger brother, Jonathan, teased her. "Right, Josie. You're the only person in the whole world that God forgot about."

I asked Josie to pull out her phone, open her Bible app, and read Romans 8:38–39. As she read the verses aloud, we could see a sense of peace wash over her. "Honey, if God keeps His Word, what is that verse telling you?"

"It's telling me God never loses His sunglasses," she said. "Or me!" She paused and finished. "Dad, I guess we could call this a Theology of Sunglasses!"

Let Us Pray

Gracious God, how grateful I am to rest secure
in Your grip forever. Amen.

Further Reflection

JOHN 10:27–29 (NKJV)

My sheep hear My voice, and I know them, and they follow Me. And I give them eternal life, and they shall never perish; neither shall anyone snatch them out of My hand. My Father, who has given them to Me, is greater than all; and no one is able to snatch them out of My Father's hand.

In His Presence

REBECCA ONDOV

My Presence will go with you,
and I will give you rest.

EXODUS 33:14 (NIV)

Sunrise, my golden retriever, paced the concrete floor. I groaned and pulled the sleeping bag over my shoulders. I hadn't gotten a good night's sleep in months. Every night my mind whirled like a tornado over the details of having a cottage built on my farm. Tonight I'd decided to get away by having a "campout" in the tack room of my barn. But Sunrise refused to lie down and sleep.

A blinding flash of lightning pierced the dark night, followed by grumbling thunder. Shaking with fear, Sunrise nuzzled me. I stroked her head. This freak lightning storm had come out of nowhere, and it rumbled for hours. *God, I need some sleep.* Sunrise bumped me with her nose. I flipped the light and slipped on my shoes. "OK, I'll take you out."

I grabbed a flashlight as Sunrise bounded out the door, raced to my Subaru, and stared at the hatch, as if to say, "I'm ready to go home now."

I rubbed my forehead. "Sunrise, we are home. This is where we're going to live. C'mon, let's go to bed." Sunrise sulked behind me.

I pulled my sleeping bag and pad off the cot and onto the floor. Sunrise wiggled next to me as I crawled into my floor-bed. As soon as I draped my arm over her, I felt her body quit quaking. Suddenly, it didn't matter where on earth she was. She quit fretting because she was in my presence. *Hmm, that's my answer too.* While in the middle of life's storms, I needed to rest in His presence. We both slept peacefully the rest of the night.

Let Us Pray

Lord, thank You for being with me every moment of every day—and every night. Amen.

Further Reflection

HEBREWS 4:1 (NIV)

Therefore, since the promise of entering his rest still stands, let us be careful that none of you be found to have fallen short of it.

1 JOHN 3:19 (NIV)

This is how we know that we belong to the truth and how we set our hearts at rest in his presence.

Healing Happens

SABRA CIANCANELLI

The LORD is close to the brokenhearted and saves those who are crushed in spirit.

PSALM 34:18 (NIV)

I explored the map of Hudson, New York, on my computer, zooming in on the address of my appointment. I'd purposely stayed away from Hudson because it had been my nephew's home and driving through triggered my grief.

Switching the setting from the illustrated map to street view, I looked for a good place to park. Street view is amazing. A moment captured—with people on the street, cars traveling, people walking dogs—a frozen piece of time that can be zoomed in and explored. On the corner, I noticed a blurry figure in the distance. For a second, the posture, the height, I thought, *Wait. Is that him? My nephew, Jeremy?*

Jeremy had lived only a block or two away. It was entirely possible that it was him. Closer zooming didn't help because the figure was too blurred to tell, but then it occurred to me, *If this isn't him, his picture could still be here.*

For a few hours that day, crazy as it sounds, I found peace virtually zooming up and down streets looking for my nephew in the panoramic photos that were taken years ago. I think it was the possibility that I might see him again, and that feeling was beautiful and exactly what I needed.

Grief has many stages—five that have been widely documented—but I believe there are an infinite number, as unique as each relationship, some as odd and fleeting as searching for a loved one on virtual maps. Yet somehow by the grace of God, healing happens. One step at a time, peace comes.

Let Us Pray

Heavenly Father, grief is complicated and different for everyone. Help me and all those struggling through the process. Help us find peace.

Further Reflection

PSALM 55:22 (NIV)

Cast your cares on the LORD and he will sustain you; he will never let the righteous be shaken.

REVELATION 21:4 (NIV)

He will wipe every tear from their eyes. There will be no more death or mourning or crying or pain, for the old order of things has passed away.

Listening to the Lord

JACQUELINE F. WHEELOCK

"Martha, Martha," the Lord answered, "you are worried and upset about many things, but few things are needed.... Mary has chosen what is better."

LUKE 10:41–42 (NIV)

My mind churned with my never-ending to-do list. At the very top was that insatiable chore called grocery shopping. Not thinking of the many souls who would love to have the means to buy a fraction of what I would purchase that day, I asked myself, "Didn't I just do this?" When would it ever end?

Coming dangerously close to resentment, I wondered, *Where is the rest God promised?* On that wintry morning, my endless scroll of duties—grocery shopping, phone calls, even mission work—seemingly defied what I longed for from God, but that same God quickly admonished me with a lesson I'd learned before. Chores went more smoothly when I was at peace. True rest rose and fell with my peace quotient.

Martha's complaint to Jesus about the domestic duties she carried while her sister, Mary, sat at His feet surfaced in my thoughts. "Upset by many things," Martha, too, needed that "better" part of rest called peace, not as the world gives—not that recliner, novel-reading rest I craved—but inner peace that causes us to count our blessings even as we fight supermarket-aisle traffic. The kind of rest that descended during the holiday season when I crocheted caps for the homeless and ended each day of it feeling blessed, not spent.

The rest God promises has less to do with our physical bodies and more to do with His eternal love. Godly women both, Mary understood this, while Martha was still learning. Yet no matter which sister we identify with, the key is listening to the Lord who reveals to us what is truly needed and what it takes to obtain rest.

Let Us Pray

Dear Savior, please sharpen my hearing
toward the better part.

Further Reflection

COLOSSIANS 3:14 (ESV)

And above all these put on love, which binds everything together in perfect harmony.

Promise and Hope

JOLYNDA STRANDBERG

He will wipe away every tear from their eyes, and death shall be no more, neither shall there be mourning, nor crying, nor pain anymore, for the former things have passed away.

REVELATION 21:4 (ESV)

From the kitchen, I heard Jacques say, "PawPaw, do you want to buy a rock?"

"Let me see," said PawPaw.

Over the course of PawPaw's last year, this was a common exchange between my four-year-old, Jacques, and PawPaw, which revolved around PawPaw's impressive rock collection from around the country; they often played "rock store." My heart always melted during these exchanges because my own childhood was filled with the same memories. Inevitably, we always seemed to bring home a few rocks after each visit.

Not long after this exchange and on the sad day PawPaw died, I suggested to JoElla, my daughter, and Jacques they paint one of PawPaw's rocks to place in his casket. When I returned from work that day, I found an oval rock with two sides painted; one side had a very detectable nine-year-old rainbow, and the other side had a four-year-old abstract rainbow. I was surprised that both children chose to paint the symbol of God's fidelity and covenant, a rainbow. It was just a simple rock, but it exuded promise and hope.

As the rock was placed in my grandfather's hands for burial, I knew my children's gesture was without doubt the work of our Lord in their hearts. On a day marred in grief, sorrow, and tears, two little children brought the generosity, peace, and hope of the Lord's love and promise to a family who was grieving and struggling.

Let Us Pray

Lord of comfort, help us to recognize You in those around us—in their deeds, words, and love. Amen.

Further Reflection

LAMENTATIONS 3:51 (ESV)

My eyes cause me grief at the fate of all the daughters of my city.

MATTHEW 5:4 (ESV)

Blessed are those who mourn, for they shall be comforted.

2 CORINTHIANS 7:10 (ESV)

For godly grief produces a repentance that leads to salvation without regret, whereas worldly grief produces death.

Tending the Spirit

BILL GIOVANNETTI

He shall be like a tree planted by the rivers of water, That brings forth its fruit in its season, Whose leaf also shall not wither; And whatever he does shall prosper.

PSALM 1:3 (NKJV)

"Why do they call it a weed whacker," I said to Margi, "when I'm the one who gets whacked?" She laughed as I peeled off my flannel shirt, splattered with burrs and the residue of chopped-up weeds. Our 3-acre property is set in a verdant valley. Home to wildlife and wildflowers, with rolling hills beside us and purple mountains in the distance, our little plot of land couldn't be prettier.

Nor could it be a better host for weeds. Invasive species, like star thistle, had proliferated after our wildfires. It was my chore to weed-whack them into oblivion. I took every precaution for the all-day job. Eye protection, face protection, hat, earplugs, high boots, jeans, leather gloves, and a long-sleeved shirt. It had been a long while since the last time I attacked those weeds.

Normally, I enjoy yard work, but not this time. The temperature hit triple digits and the sun was relentless. Clothed head to toe, I was a hot mess. I was a mess in my heart too. I'd been letting discontent take root. I fretted over unanswered prayers, the demands of life, and a schedule I let get away from me.

I was glad to be finished with the weeds. "It's a lot easier when I don't let them grow this big," I said.

My wife nodded as she helped me pull my boots off. "Isn't it that way with everything?"

Her words touched my heart. I'd been letting weeds grow in my spirit, and it was time to get to them before they got too big.

Let Us Pray

Lord, teach me to tend every day the garden of faith, hope, and love in my soul. Amen.

Further Reflection

HOSEA 14:5 (NKJV)

I will be like the dew to Israel; He shall grow like the lily, And lengthen his roots like Lebanon.

The Promise of Rest

PATTY KIRK

We do not know what we ought to pray for, but the Spirit himself intercedes for us through wordless groans.

ROMANS 8:26 (NIV)

My husband, Kris, had a heart attack this spring. Shortly after we went to the emergency room, they wheeled him off for surgery.

You might guess I was in constant prayer from that moment onward, but I'm ashamed to say I wasn't. I couldn't pray at all.

Our church pastor came at six the morning of the surgery. Kris was being prepped, and I was trying to keep out of the way of technicians shaving his chest and nurses in green masks fiddling with his IVs. We three held hands, and Pastor Mike prayed. I said amen at the end but only out of politeness. With so much happening, I was too agitated to actually pray.

What's wrong with me? I wondered after they wheeled Kris away. I chatted with Mike and my boss for hours in the waiting room. A friend took me out to dinner, and I recounted everything that had happened. But I couldn't utter or even think forth a word to the One I depended on for Kris's recovery, my salvation, everything.

After that first day, whenever I thought of praying, I fell asleep. A lifelong bad sleeper, I've never slept so deeply,

immediately, or well as at Kris's bedside: through meals, nurses replacing IV bags and taking blood, doctors visiting, machines beeping.

You're worse than those disciples at Gethsemane, I accused myself. *Your flesh weak, your spirit nonexistent.*

But the rest I was getting—so restorative in those hard days of worry!—felt so blessed. And God promises rest to those who love him. Evidently, despite my inability to pray, God attended not only to Kris but also to me, restoring me with sleep.

Let Us Pray

Thank You, Father, for accepting me even when
I don't reach out to You in prayer.

Further Reflection

MATTHEW 11:28–30 (NIV)

Come to me, all you who are weary and burdened, and I will give you rest. Take my yoke upon you and learn from me, for I am gentle and humble in heart, and you will find rest for your souls. For my yoke is easy and my burden is light.

Lesson from a Robin

PENNEY SCHWAB

Are not two sparrows sold for a penny?
Yet not one of them will fall to the
ground outside your Father's care.

MATTHEW 10:29 (NIV)

The back porch door was only open for a few seconds, but that was time enough for a half-grown robin to fly down the hall and into our laundry room. The poor bird frantically circled the room, wings beating hard. I knew it was scared, but what to do? I tried capturing it in a large towel but couldn't get close. Trapping it in the corner with my broom didn't work either.

My husband, Don, squeezed through the door. "Stop trying to catch it!" he said. "When the bird tires, it will land on a shelf and I'll get it." A couple of minutes later, that's what happened. Don picked the robin up, carried it outside, and watched it fly to the nearest Bradford pear tree.

I hate to admit it, but I'm a lot like that bird. My initial reaction to unsettling news or a troubling circumstance is panic.

I rush around and try to fix things that don't need fixing or aren't my business. Often my hasty "solutions" to problems don't even make sense, such as the time my granddaughter Olivia was driving alone and had a flat tire ninety miles away. My plan was to go pick her up, but Don said, "Why not call a garage to fix the tire?" I did, and Olivia was back on the road in forty-five minutes.

These days, I'm trying to remember that robin when I receive bad news or encounter stressful situations. With God's help, I'm learning to take a deep breath, stay calm, wait awhile, and trust that He will provide appropriate help in every situation.

Let Us Pray

Lord, You have told us to learn from the birds of the air (Matthew 6:26). Let it be so in my life. Amen.

Further Reflection

ISAIAH 41:10 (NIV)

So do not fear, for I am with you; do not be dismayed, for I am your God. I will strengthen you and help you; I will uphold you with my righteous right hand.

JAMES 5:7–8 (NIV)

Be patient, then, brothers and sisters, until the Lord's coming. See how the farmer waits for the land to yield its valuable crop, patiently waiting for the autumn and spring rains. You too, be patient and stand firm, because the Lord's coming is near.

Pray for Me

KIM TAYLOR HENRY

The eternal God is your refuge, and his everlasting arms are under you.

DEUTERONOMY 33:27 (NLT)

The doctor who was about to replace my hip bone with a manufactured one came into the pre-op room. "Are you nervous?" he asked.

"Yes."

"Me too," he joked, signing his initials on my right thigh.

I smiled and tried to relax. I'd fought this hip replacement for three years, until the pain became too limiting. Now here I was; there was no turning back. I had confidence in my doctor. Most of all, I had confidence in my Lord. I repeated Psalm 28:7 (NLT): "The Lord is my strength and shield. I trust him with all my heart."

After two hours, I was out of surgery. Everything went well; now I needed to recover. The next two weeks passed in a fog of painkillers and sleep. I stayed focused on just getting through.

Normally I talk with God throughout the day. Now I was acutely aware of my need for Him but unable to gather my thoughts. How would I get through if I couldn't even pray? Then one day, lying in my study, it hit me: my family and friends were doing the praying that I could not. Their prayers, not mine, would make the difference. Peace instantly filled me.

Let Us Pray

Lord, thank You that when I'm too weak to even pray,
I have the prayers of others and Your everlasting arms.

Further Reflection

PSALM 42:1–2, 5 (NLT)

As the deer longs for streams of water, so I long for you,
O God. I thirst for God, the living God. When can I go
and stand before him?...Why am I discouraged? Why is
my heart so sad? I will put my hope in God! I will praise
him again.

ISAIAH 46:4 (NLT)

I will be your God throughout your lifetime—until your hair
is white with age. I made you, and I will care for you. I will
carry you along and save you.

On the Run

MARCI ALBORGHETTI

Jacob ... lay down ... And he dreamed that there was a ladder set up on the earth, the top of it reaching to heaven; and the angels of God were ascending and descending on it. And the LORD stood beside him.

GENESIS 28:10–13 (NRSV)

Whenever I read this scripture, I feel jealous of Jacob. What I wouldn't give to close my eyes to seek rest and have God send a dream to comfort me! My rest is, as often as not, an epic struggle between a too-vivid imagination and a perpetually anxious mind. When the two sides stop their tug-of-war and start working together, it's even worse.

Just as Jacob was on the run from Esau, the brother he had wronged, I am sometimes on the run from worries and problems when I lie down to sleep. I don't always go to bed expecting peace or that God will give me rest, and a dream I had recently makes me wonder if my perspective is the real problem.

I dreamed that I was running laps in a strange place, sometimes on a path, sometimes on a road. The entire dream consisted of my running. When I awakened, I automatically started down the "poor me" path because of another night of restlessness and exhausting dreams.

Then I noticed how I felt: Good! Awake! Energetic! So I started thinking about the dream. How had I really felt during it? Alive, optimistic, strong, amazed that I could keep running. And in my amazement, I'd realized that there was no way I was running so strongly and well on my own; God was giving me the strength.

For the first time after one of my seemingly exhausting dreams, I was fully rested.

Let Us Pray

Oh, God, help me recognize that I can always access Your comfort, waking or dreaming, if I just remember to shift my perspective. Amen.

Further Reflection

GENESIS 28:16 (NRSV)

Then Jacob woke from his sleep and said, "Surely the LORD is in this place—and I did not know it!"

PSALM 32:6–7 (NRSV)

Therefore let all who are faithful offer prayer to you; at a time of distress, the rush of mighty waters shall not reach them. You are a hiding place for me; you preserve me from trouble; you surround me with glad cries of deliverance. Selah.

Life Is a Prayer

JIM HINCH

Holy, holy, holy is the LORD of hosts;
the whole earth is full of his glory.

ISAIAH 6:3 (NRSV)

The wind shook my tent. It poked sharp fingers into my sleeping bag. I was camped on snow beside an alpine lake in Yosemite. The snow had fallen the night before and more was expected. A layer of fresh powder blanketed the peaks around me, glowing eerily in the moonlight. The temperature was below freezing and falling.

But I wasn't worried. I sensed God in all of it—the snow, the wind, the cold. So I lay curled for warmth, at peace.

How different from a year ago! I'd hiked this very same trail, solo like now, and I'd been anxious the whole time. It was balmy then, dry as a bone. But I'd been preoccupied, worried about work, pestering God to give me some clear guidance about the future. The louder I raised my voice in prayer, the less I seemed to hear.

This time I tried a different approach. I remembered something a wise friend said: "All of life can be prayer if you let it."

I let my boots hitting the trail be prayer. The dense pines at the trailhead and the rockscapes above the tree line. My tired muscles. My hunger at dinner. The silence of the lake reflecting snow. The moon. The stars. And now the cold and the wind.

It worked. Looking patiently for God in the landscape, I saw Him. Listening for His voice without the noise of my own demands, I heard Him. And seeing Him, hearing Him, I felt His peace in a way I'd never experienced before.

I curled up tighter. I couldn't sleep in this cold wind. But I didn't want to. I was in God's presence. I would savor every moment.

Let Us Pray

I'll let You do the talking when I pray today, Lord. Speak to me in the beauty of Your creation.

Further Reflection

PSALM 24:1–2 (NRSV)

The earth is the LORD's and all that is in it, the world, and those who live in it; for he has founded it on the seas, and established it on the rivers.

ZEPHANIAH 1:7 (NRSV)

Be silent before the Lord God! For the day of the Lord is at hand; the Lord has prepared a sacrifice, he has consecrated his guests.

Ask and You Shall Receive

ERIN MacPHERSON

Look to the LORD and his strength;
seek his face always.

1 CHRONICLES 16:11 (NIV)

"Will you please pray for me right now?" my friend Sam texted in her moment of distress.

"I'm on it!" I replied before setting aside my phone to continue making dinner. I pulled out a carrot from the refrigerator and began to peel it, thinking about how Sam's husband had lost his job and they were struggling to buy groceries. Next came tomatoes, and I considered how hard it must be for Sam to watch her husband apply for job after job only to be turned down. Then I added an avocado and some lettuce. I finished up the salad and picked up my phone to see another text from Sam. "I'm really struggling. Life feels so heavy."

I swallowed a lump of guilt. I had promised to pray but instead made salad and allowed my mind to be carried away with my own thoughts. My friend needed to be in front of God, whom she so desperately needed.

I headed to the couch, where I got down on my knees and lifted Sam and her family up to God. I pleaded with Him to bring her peace and clarity as they figured out the next steps. I prayed that God would bring her hope that went beyond human understanding, so she could walk forward and trust Him to provide even when things seemed dire.

Another text came: "Peace has calmed my soul, my desperation is gone, my hope has been reclaimed."

We need only to ask—not think, not meddle, not solve, not talk—and our great, powerful, all-knowing Provider will do the rest.

Let Us Pray

Lord, draw my eyes toward You and my knees to the floor when my loved ones need You most. Amen.

Further Reflection

ROMANS 8:26 (NIV)

In the same way, the Spirit helps us in our weakness. We do not know what we ought to pray for, but the Spirit himself intercedes for us through wordless groans.

In His Arms

SHAWNELLE ELIASEN

On the day I called, you answered me; my strength of soul you increased.

PSALM 138:3 (ESV)

Mama, can I climb up?" Isaiah asked. We were deep into the night, and the bedroom was dark as pitch. But I heard my little son and pushed back the covers to welcome him.

He had a fever. Heat radiated through his pajamas. It seeped from his skin. "Where do you hurt?" I whispered.

"My throat. My head. My legs," he said.

I knew I'd move from the bed in a moment. Isaiah needed a fever reducer and a drink. But I paused for just a pulse of time because my son had settled in. His body curled against mine, and we fit perfectly. It came to mind, as we lay in midnight hues, that when he formed and grew under my heart, together our curve was convex. Now, we were concave. As he nestled against me, he fit into my hollow places; we were so close we were like one again. He was in need and found his way to me.

It was the same way that I'd gone to God so many times recently. Helpless. Hurting. Needing love, care, mercy, and grace. I curled into Him. Rested in His shelter. Listened for His heartbeat—the perfect cadence that brings peace to pain. In His arms, I found restoration and healing. Time and time again.

Isaiah whimpered softly, and it was time for me to slide from bed. I'd meet his needs. I wanted to love and comfort and care for my precious child with all that I am. And my God does the same for me.

Let Us Pray

**Thank You, Lord, for caring for me when
I'm hurting. Amen.**

Further Reflection

PSALM 147:3 (ESV)

He heals the brokenhearted and binds up their wounds.

2 CORINTHIANS 4:16 (ESV)

So we do not lose heart. Though our outer self is wasting away, our inner self is being renewed day by day.

ISAIAH 33:2 (NIV)

LORD, be gracious to us; we long for you. Be our strength every morning, our salvation in time of distress.

Clean Slate

PAM KIDD

And know . . .

PSALM 46:10 (KJV)

For several days, I'd noticed a tattoo on our contractor's arm. I recognized it as a Latin phrase but had no idea what it meant. He had come to us highly recommended and was making some repairs on our house. He was a fine craftsman, meticulous in his work. Finally, on a morning break, I gathered the nerve to ask, "So what does the tattoo say?"

"*Tabula Rasa* . . . clean slate," he answered.

Clean slate. I smiled, remembering when Brock was a fifth-grader with a bad case of being "all boy." I would tuck him in each night with the same reassurance: "Tomorrow's a new day. The slate is wiped clean."

Some of us are fortunate. Our past infractions aren't bad enough to put us in jail or require extensive rehabilitation. Some of us have experienced pain, discouragement, and hurt so severe we have succumbed to drugs or alcohol or violence. But there's one thing we all have in common. If we look for God, even in our darkest times, we'll find He's very near . . . already busy wiping our slates clean.

I went out on the deck to think about the tattoo. The day was clear. A cardinal was singing on a nearby tree. I had a sense that looking for God and knowing He's near wasn't quite enough. I had to do my part by meeting Him. The clean slate was just the beginning.

As I stood in the cool of the day, with the sun warming my skin, I felt all of my "if onlys" and "I should haves" melting away. Not only does God deliver a clean slate anytime we ask, He follows up by offering the profound peace of the present moment: "Stop. Be still. Know Me."

Let Us Pray

I find You in the stillness, Father. Somehow I know You are there.

Further Reflection

PSALM 119:18 (NRSV)

Open my eyes, so that I may behold wondrous things out of your law.

ISAIAH 40:28 (NRSV)

Have you not known? Have you not heard? The LORD is the everlasting God, the Creator of the ends of the earth. He does not faint or grow weary; his understanding is unsearchable.

ISAIAH 41:10 (NRSV)

Do not fear, for I am with you, do not be afraid, for I am your God; I will strengthen you, I will help you, I will uphold you with my victorious right hand.

Unexpected Moments

SABRA CIANCANELLI

*On the day the LORD gave the Amorites
into the power of Israel, Joshua spoke to the
LORD... "Sun, stand still at Gibeon! and
Moon, at the Aijalon Valley!" The sun stood
still and the moon stood motionless until a
nation took revenge on its enemies.*

JOSHUA 10:12–13 (CEB)

Our telescope is down from the loft in the barn, set up on
the lawn, and positioned at a perfect angle to the sky. The
boys want me to wake them if there's a good view. My husband
snores, and I am watching the clock, which reads 3:05. Outside
a rare lunar eclipse is happening.

I stare into the darkness, searching for the "blood moon"
that the news has hyped, but it's obscured by a blanket of
clouds. I look and look, waiting for a break, a slight glimpse
of the phenomenon, and I think of Joshua's prayer for the

sun to stand still—an impossible prayer that was answered nonetheless.

I look into the early morning sky and think of the many impossible prayers I've prayed staring out this bedroom window during dark times in my life, when fear and worries about health and family kept me awake.

Right now is different. I'm overcome by how peaceful it is, how grateful I am to be here, enjoying this sacred space, this darkness. And even though I'm missing the celestial event, I feel close, so very close, to God, as if anything is possible, as if a miracle is happening—and it is.

Let Us Pray

Heavenly Father, thank You for this beautiful, unexpected moment of knowing Your incredible love in the deepest places of my heart.

Further Reflection

ROMANS 8:37–39 (CEB)

But in all these things we win a sweeping victory through the one who loved us. I'm convinced that nothing can separate us from God's love in Christ Jesus our Lord: not death or life, not angels or rulers, not present things or future things, not powers or height or depth, or any other thing that is created.

1 JOHN 3:1 (CEB)

See what kind of love the Father has given to us in that we should be called God's children, and that is what we are! Because the world didn't recognize him, it doesn't recognize us.

Good for the Soul

MARK COLLINS

The wilderness and the wasteland shall be glad for them, And the desert shall rejoice and blossom as the rose.

ISAIAH 35:1 (NKJV)

I'm standing at the edge of the Kubuqi Desert in Inner Mongolia, holding a shovel. I'm part of the University of Pittsburgh's contingent to Future Forests, a Chinese/Korean/American student project aimed at combating the spreading desert by planting hundreds of thousands of trees—an undertaking that will go on for years, maybe decades. We're here at the invitation of former South Korean Ambassador Kwon Byong Hyon, the founder of Future Forest and a loyal Pitt grad.

This is hard work. To secure the newly planted trees against the relentless wind, you first affix a square wooden framework in the sand. Each frame is homemade—a cluster of sticks tied together with twine and embedded into the plot. Before me are scores of students kneeling, hats tied under their chins and bandannas around their mouths to shield against the blowing sand, deftly tying twigs together, digging holes, planting, watering, starting again.

Standing back, taking in the larger, breathtaking picture, makes this venture seem fruitless. Could hundreds (thousands, millions) of trees really stop a relentless desert, whose ever-shifting, ever-expanding sand blows thousands of miles,

adding to the pollution woes of cities like Beijing, sometimes all the way to Seoul?

But that's not what I see. I see commitment against the wind, the odds. With their bandannas pulled high and hats pulled low, it's impossible to tell who's Chinese or Korean or American. And whoever is looking down upon us as we hurtle through space, third rock from the sun, sees the same thing: a bevy of young people laboring together to make a desert blossom. It's work that's good for Seoul. It's good for any soul.

Let Us Pray

Lord, lift the veil from our eyes and let us see what You see: people as people, in unity and peace.

Further Reflection

DEUTERONOMY 32:10 (NKJV)

He found him in a desert land And in the wasteland, a howling wilderness; He encircled him, He instructed him, He kept him as the apple of His eye.

JOB 24:5 (NKJV)

Indeed, like wild donkeys in the desert, They go out to their work, searching for food. The wilderness yields food for them and for their children.

Turning My Eyes to the Lord

ERIKA BENTSEN

The heavens declare the glory of God;
And the firmament shows His handiwork.

PSALM 19:1 (NKJV)

What a rotten day," I growled at the darkness, lit only by my headlights on the narrow, windy mountain road. I was driving back to the family ranch, thirty-five miles from town, after an extremely stressful meeting. I slouched in the seat, letting my worries hang around my shoulders like an anchor. "This is horrible, Lord," I prayed or, rather, complained. "What a terrible world this is."

I rounded a corner and, lo, before me was the moon, so full and large it seemed to pervade the whole sky. Moonlight reflected in a nearby stream, turning it into glowing silver as it zigzagged in a shimmering path across an open field.

It took my breath away. I was in the middle of God's majestic handiwork. The seemingly monumental weight of my burdens vanished in the awesome splendor of the painted landscape. *What can mere man do that is more powerful or can last longer than this?* I thought. Even though my problems had felt enormous, God was bigger and far more powerful.

My worries evaporated. Just as the moonlight filled the quiet stream with an overflowing glow, God's peaceful beauty replenished my troubled heart with overflowing joy. I needed only to look around to remember He was everlasting and only a prayer away.

Let Us Pray

Lord, "I will lift up mine eyes unto the hills, from whence cometh my help" (Psalm 121:1, KJV).

Further Reflection

PSALM 24:7 (NKJV)

Lift up your heads, O you gates! And be lifted up, you everlasting doors! And the King of glory shall come in.

PSALM 150:2 (NKJV)

Praise Him for His mighty acts; Praise Him according to His excellent greatness!

LUKE 9:43 (NKJV)

And they were all amazed at the majesty of God. But while everyone marveled at all the things which Jesus did, He said to His disciples.

Firm Footing

JULIA ATTAWAY

They prayed for the new believers there
that they might receive the Holy Spirit.

ACTS 8:15 (NIV)

An acquaintance sought me out at a big event and pulled
me outside. She'd helped plan the party. "I feel lousy!" she
sobbed. "I've worked so hard, and everyone seems to be mad at
me about something."

I hugged her tightly and said all the reassuring things I
could think of, starting with how it was a truly beautiful event
that showed lots of work and planning and finishing by noting
that people often say harsh things whenever they care deeply
because they want everything to be perfect.

"I know." My friend sniffled. "But I grew up in a family of
alcoholics, and when things get stressful, I try to take control.
And then everyone gets angry at me."

I absorbed that news. With my children and spouse, mood
disorders and anxiety cause things to spin out of control. I
know all too well the temptation to impose order on chaos by
becoming authoritative. I've learned the hard way that it's wiser
to be flexible than controlling.

As gently as I could, I offered, "Breathe deeply and find your
grounding. You only need to control what's under your control.
Remember what you believe in and hold it close."

"But I don't know what I believe!" she wailed.

"Breathe deeply and you'll remember," I replied. She did and, in a few minutes, was more peaceful.

She thanked me and wiped her eyes. "I wish I had the kind of grounding you seem to have," she said.

It wasn't the time or place for a theological discussion, so I sent up a prayer on her behalf. "You'll get there. Just keep searching for the truth . . . and then build your life around it."

Let Us Pray

Holy Spirit, enter the hearts and minds of those who don't know You and kindle in them the fire of Your love.

Further Reflection

JOHN 6:35, 40 (NIV)

Then Jesus declared, "I am the bread of life. Whoever comes to me will never go hungry, and whoever believes in me will never be thirsty. For my Father's will is that everyone who looks to the Son and believes in him shall have eternal life, and I will raise them up at the last day."

Never Letting Go

ERIN MacPHERSON

*Shout aloud and sing for joy, people
of Zion, for great is the Holy
One of Israel among you.*

ISAIAH 12:6 (NIV)

She doesn't remember that we talked just five minutes ago, that she told me it had been raining all day and she was enjoying a cup of tea by the fire. So we have the conversation again, raindrops beating against the window, providing a calming cadence to soothe my anxious heart.

"Well, goodbye, Erin. We'll talk again soon."

"Goodbye, Grandma. I love you!" I hang up the phone, a lump catching in my throat at the sound of my name. At least she still remembers me—for now.

Tears come, and I remember the good times: mornings on her cattle ranch, helping her toss hay out of the tractor; long afternoons picking buckets of blueberries in the sunshine;

comforting hugs; gentle prayers. They are a spiritual heritage I am grateful for to this day.

The phone's ring jerks me out of my reverie. "Oh, hi, Grandma!"

"Erin, how are you? It's raining here, but I'm still having a lovely day."

"Oh, Grandma, I'm so glad."

She pauses. "Erin, God is just filling me with His presence today, as if the only thing that can bring me contentment is Him."

There it was: something different, something real, a glimmer of the person she once was. Yes, she is slowly and terribly losing her mind and the memories that had taken a lifetime to build, but God isn't letting go. Instead, He clings to her and fills her with blessed contentment even when all else is gone.

Let Us Pray

Lord Jesus, fill my soul with the joy that can come only from You until the very end of my days. Amen.

Further Reflection

PSALM 27:6 (NIV)

Then my head will be exalted above the enemies who surround me; at his sacred tent I will sacrifice with shouts of joy; I will sing and make music to the LORD.

JOHN 16:22 (NIV)

So with you: Now is your time of grief, but I will see you again and you will rejoice, and no one will take away your joy.

The Promise

PATTY KIRK

*The promise is for you and your children
and for all who are far off—for all
whom the Lord our God will call.*

ACTS 2:39 (NIV)

Today, on the phone, my former student Ali spoke of my daughters as "children of the covenant."

"What does that mean?" I asked her. Homeschooled by missionary parents, Ali often speaks a language I don't understand.

"Oh, you know. You've raised your girls in a Jesus-loving household. Now it's up to God." Ali was telling me to trust in God's promise, something I struggled with.

We'd been talking about a fantasy I have: that the older my daughters get, the closer I will be to contentment. In my shimmering vision, they love God, are in happy relationships, fulfilled in their jobs, living in clean houses, and raising healthy children with parental confidence and foresight I never experienced. But the older my daughters get, the further away this heavenly vision seems.

Sometimes I think this fantasy is my main impediment to contentment. After all, my home is fairly clean; I love God and my husband and my work; my girls are healthy and thriving and occasionally kindhearted and God-oriented. Still, I'm anything but content when I start worrying about them.

God and every angel who ever visited Earth commands, "Fear not!" I long to obey, but how does one shut down this particular worry?

Today, considering God's many pledges of love to us, I suddenly resaw my fantasy as God's too: what we want for our children is what He wants for us. With one difference: God has the power to make it happen.

Let Us Pray

Father, Abba, Daddy, we are the children of Your hopes and many promises, the children of Your power and love. Let everything happen according to Your good purposes.

Further Reflection

PROVERBS 22:6 (NIV)

Start children off on the way they should go, and even when they are old they will not turn from it.

ISAIAH 54:9–10 (NIV)

"To me this is like the days of Noah, when I swore that the waters of Noah would never again cover the earth. So now I have sworn not to be angry with you, never to rebuke you again. Though the mountains be shaken and the hills be removed, yet my unfailing love for you will not be shaken nor my covenant of peace be removed," says the LORD.

The Sound of Hope

SHAWNELLE ELIASEN

*I will hope continually and will
praise you yet more and more.*

PSALM 71:14 (ESV)

Hey, Mom, want to hear what I've been working on?" my
son asked. I nodded, and we headed to the family room.
He took a seat on the piano bench, as I sat on the sofa by the
fireplace, and he began to play.

This music wasn't a song yet, just a melody. But the rhythm
reached my soul. I watched my boy. He was near adult age, and
the growing years also grew distance between us. We've struggled. And when one member of the family hurts, all do. We're
connected by love.

As I listened to my son play, I noticed his hands. I remembered when they laced with mine. When his fingers first curled
around a pencil and later the steering wheel of my car. I ad-
mired his profile. With a few notes, the years washed away. I
was looking at my robust, full-of-life little boy.

This invitation was everything. It was more than the beginning of a song. Finally, my son had invited me into a tender part
of his life. The place where music lives and creativity runs free.
A gentle place. A place of peace. I closed my eyes and thanked
the Lord for this goodness. I thanked Him for this moment
when worry was suspended and His love penetrated like heat
from the hearth. God was reaching into my son's life. Pursuing

him. Drawing him. That night, the Lord allowed a glimpse of His presence. A moment to breathe and be warmed by His glory.

The Lord loved this child. This child was His own.

My son stopped playing. I wanted to fill the space with a thousand words, but I shared only two.

"It's beautiful."

He smiled and moved his fingers over the keys again.

To me, this was the sound of hope.

Let Us Pray

Lord, You are the pursuer of hearts and saver of souls. In You is every hope. Amen.

Further Reflection

ROMANS 12:1 (ESV)

I appeal to you therefore, brothers, by the mercies of God, to present your bodies as a living sacrifice, holy and acceptable to God, which is your spiritual worship.

ROMANS 15:13 (ESV)

May the God of hope fill you with all joy and peace in believing, so that by the power of the Holy Spirit you may abound in hope.

PSALM 33:18 (ESV)

Behold, the eye of the LORD is on those who fear him, on those who hope in his steadfast love.

A Staycation with God

MARCI ALBORGHETTI

"Keeping covenant and steadfast love— do not treat lightly all the hardship that has come upon us."

NEHEMIAH 9:32 (NRSV)

I can't do this," I said, looking up at my husband, Charlie, from the floor where I was zipping my suitcase closed.

We were due to head to the airport for our annual four-month winter sojourn in California from Connecticut. But I'd gotten sick, and now, despite my doctor's assurances that I could travel, I still felt lousy.

Charlie looked relieved but uncertain. "You sure?" he asked.

"Yes, I just can't. I'm sorry."

Charlie and I had started taking these trips eight years ago when he had partly retired, fearing he'd be lured back into the ninety-hour workweeks that had caused grief in our marriage.

Surely we could find a way to stay home, still have some of the fun we'd found in California, and negotiate between my need for privacy and Charlie's social nature.

While unpacking, I felt panic rising. *Will this hurt our marriage?*

I went to find Charlie. He was on the couch, phone in hand. He looked up a little sheepishly. I sat down next to him, we clasped hands, and I prayed: "Lord, help us to use this time to grow closer to You and to each other. Bless and protect our marriage. Amen."

Charlie turned off the phone, and I looked at the silver river outside our window. A peace stole over me. God had brought us through so much together; I would trust Him now.

Let Us Pray

God of all circumstances, help us to know
we are where You want us to be.

Further Reflection

JOB 38:4 (NRSV)

Where were you when I laid the foundation of the earth?
Tell me, if you have understanding.

An Open Heart

EVELYN BENCE

The LORD thy God is with thee whithersoever thou goest.

JOSHUA 1:9 (KJV)

I'll admit it: for years, I've been a nervous driver. Bridges. Mountains. Wet roads. Parking garages. Narrow streets. Interstates. Rush-hour crush. Any number of scenarios make me grit my teeth as I grip the wheel. My tension abates as I ease off the gas, coasting into my own street.

Home and safe, I thought, sighing, on a recent evening. Setting down my umbrella, I glanced at the ceramic plaque hung years ago right inside my front door: "Peace be with you." In my decorative scheme, its message was meant for visitors. But as I turned the lock and settled in for the night, I claimed the motto for myself, here in my home, within my sturdy brick walls.

Later in the week, a young neighbor girl, who struggles to read and whose family speaks Spanish, stopped in after school as she does every day. "We can talk and play for half an hour," I explained, "but then I have to go out."

As I gathered up my purse and gloves, dreading my drive toward rush-hour dusk, she stood by the door and nodded toward the plaque. "What does it say?" she asked, as if seeing it for the first time.

Drawing close and pointing out each word, I read out loud the four one-syllable words. Then I heard a second question: "What does *peace* mean?"

"Well," I proposed, "peace is the opposite of fighting, and peace is the opposite of being afraid."

Before I could think of a third explanation, she interrupted. "It means God be with you."

Was it a statement or a question? I wasn't sure. But as I reached for the doorknob, I heartily said, "Yes!"

God be with me. As I leave my own home, as I drive into the night, as my heart opens to accept His peace.

Let Us Pray

Lord, be with me today. Enfold me in Your presence. Fill me with Your peace.

Further Reflection

ISAIAH 26:3 (NIV)

You will keep in perfect peace those whose minds are steadfast, because they trust in you.

My Ever-Present Guide

ERIKA BENTSEN

*And the life which I now live in the flesh
I live by faith in the Son of God.*

GALATIANS 2:20 (NKJV)

I may never fully recover from rupturing a disk while fighting a fire on the ranch where I've worked for nineteen years. Questions flood my mind: *What's my future? Will I ever be pain-free? Will I ever ride a horse again? Can I ever ranch again?*

"I've been waiting a year for God's direction and there's no reply," I complained to my friend Lori.

"Look," she said, "maybe He's waiting for you. A compass won't budge if you're standing still. God will lead you, but maybe He wants you to begin."

In the darkness of this last year, I've had to confront my future without ranching. And, oh, has that been hard! But as I've walked this tough road, understanding that my life will never be the same, I've finally been able to surrender my ranching to God. It took time, hard prayers, and hours of weeping, but joy is starting to come in the mornings. New opportunities have flooded in: the ranch offered to buy my cows, with the hope I can buy them back one day. Doctors have come up with new theories for making me well again.

Walking in faith doesn't always lead me to where I want to go but to where God wants me. And I know I'm better off for it. However my life turns out, I am finally at peace knowing God will be there to guide me.

Let Us Pray

Lord, lead me. I'm ready now.

Further Reflection

MALACHI 4:2 (NKJV)

But to you who fear My name The Sun of Righteousness shall arise With healing in His wings; And you shall go out And grow fat like stall-fed calves.

JAMES 4:7 (NKJV)

Therefore submit to God. Resist the devil and he will flee from you.

The Great Outdoors

ERIN MacPHERSON

*It is good that one should wait quietly
for the salvation of the LORD.*

LAMENTATIONS 3:26 (ESV)

I sprawled out in the hammock, hung from two giant oaks just steps from the lake, and closed my eyes, soaking in the glory of the day. Crickets chirped. A woodpecker rattled. Tiny butterflies floated by on the breeze.

OK, they were moths. But they were still pretty. And the breeze was a bit chilly for my taste. And fleas bit my legs, reminding me that the great outdoors is called "outdoors" for a reason.

Yet still, this city girl who loves things like climate control and pest control was finding something akin to—was it peace? As I closed my eyes and took in a deep breath of the country air, my heart cried out to God. *Why is it so hard for me to just "be"? To let You fill my spirit with Your Word, life, hope, and peace? To listen to the quiet, still voice and know that You are God?*

It came like a whisper from one of the moth's wings: You don't let Me.

I had let my own thoughts interfere. I had let those pesky fleas interrupt. I had let the chilly breeze steal my peace, the peace that God so desperately wants to give me.

Let Us Pray

Speak to me, Lord, not through the noise and clutter, but through the silence. Amen.

Further Reflection

PSALM 26:2–3 (NIV)

Test me, LORD, and try me, examine my heart and my mind; for I have always been mindful of your unfailing love and have lived in reliance on your faithfulness.

MATTHEW 6:25–26 (NIV)

Therefore I tell you, do not worry about your life, what you will eat or drink; or about your body, what you will wear. Is not life more than food, and the body more than clothes? Look at the birds of the air; they do not sow or reap or store away in barns, and yet your heavenly Father feeds them. Are you not much more valuable than they?

A New Peace

JULIE GARMON

*Rejoice with an indescribable
and glorious joy.*

1 PETER 1:8 (NRSV)

A re you sure you want to do this?" I asked my daughter
Katie. "It's not too late to back out. I bet Laura would
understand."

"I'm positive, Mom."

We walked toward the pregnancy resource center together,
where my cousin Laura works. When I told Katie about my
volunteering, she said she wanted to help too. We'd spent
weeks training and were prepared, but my heart ached for my
daughter. She'd been dealing with infertility issues. Would
she be able to handle working in this atmosphere?

On our first night, Katie and I accompanied new parents
to the baby boutique to pick out clothes. As I opened the door,
the powdery scent of diapers met me. Surely, Katie noticed the
sweet smell too. *Lord, can she handle this?*

The new father gently cradled his infant daughter while the mother oohed and aahed at the rows of tiny outfits and shoes. "Your baby's beautiful," Katie said. And she was too—dark hair and eyes just like Katie's.

Katie touched the baby's head. "Let's find something really pretty for you," she suggested.

Later, I asked, "Are you OK?"

"It's harder than I thought," Katie responded, "but something amazing happens when I see mamas with their babies. I forget about myself and what I want. All I feel is joy for them."

Let Us Pray

Father, surrender brings an unexplainable peace all its own.

Further Reflection

EPHESIANS 4:2–3 (NLT)

Always be humble and gentle. Be patient with each other, making allowance for each other's faults because of your love. Make every effort to keep yourselves united in the Spirit, binding yourselves together with peace.

Giving Thanks

LISA BOGART

Rejoice always, pray continually, give thanks in all circumstances; for this is God's will for you in Christ Jesus.

1 THESSALONIANS 5:16–18 (NIV)

As I took off my sweater for the fourth time that morning, I tried to give thanks. "Thank You, God, for hot flashes." Oh, He could tell my heart was not in it. I tried again. "Thank You for the changes in my body." *Hmm. Yes. Thank You for these changes.*

I am changing, and it's rather fascinating. The last time I experienced this much physical change I was pregnant; before that, it was adolescence. "Hey, God, how cool is being human? We grow over a lifetime. You created an amazing machine!"

Another hot flash surged through me. My face flushed and my back heated up. I pulled off my sweater again. Rather than getting upset, I was intrigued by the wonder of my body. I timed the heat wave—ninety seconds. It was not nearly as long as I had thought. My annoyance faded just a little.

Being thankful in all circumstances does not mean you have to like it. Being thankful means acknowledging the situation and doing your best to give thanks. With that prayer comes a response from God, an offering of peace.

I still have hot flashes and get annoyed with the drastic change in my temperature, but when I remember to give thanks, it is easier.

Let Us Pray

Dear Father God, saying thank You is a hard discipline. Remind me that all of the circumstances in my life come from You and that I can rejoice over them. Amen.

Further Reflection

PROVERBS 3:5–6 (NIV)

Trust in the LORD with all your heart and lean not on your own understanding; in all your ways submit to him, and he will make your paths straight.

COLOSSIANS 1:11 (NIV)

…being strengthened with all power according to his glorious might so that you may have great endurance and patience.

Depositing Peace

KATIE GANSHERT

And the peace of God, which transcends all understanding, will guard your hearts and your minds in Christ Jesus.

PHILIPPIANS 4:7 (NIV)

Worry is temporary atheism," writes author Randy Alcorn.

Funny how a simple quote could result in an overwhelming flood of conviction. You see, I'd been worrying a lot, especially about adopting a little girl from the Congo. Everything that could go wrong was going wrong. Despite God's many commands not to, I was letting worry reign in my heart.

I knew it was time to wage war on my worry. If I wanted to experience that all-surpassing peace Paul talks about in Philippians 4:7, I had to live out the verse that came before it: "Do not be anxious about anything, but in every situation, by prayer and petition, with thanksgiving, present your requests to God" (Philippians 4:6, NIV). So the next day, I started a worry journal.

Every single morning for four months, I wrote a list of my worries. Then I got on my knees and, out loud, I not only gave each worry to Jesus, but I also asked Him to deposit peace and joy in the empty space that my worry left behind.

I wish I'd started this a long time ago. I'm no longer wasting energy and emotions on things I can't control. I'm truly living out Philippians 4:6, and in so doing, I'm reaping the rewards of joy and peace and an ever-increasing trust in God.

Let Us Pray

Father God, thank You for the truth of Your Word and for the reward that comes when I live out those truths.

Further Reflection

PSALM 55:22 (NIV)

Cast your cares on the LORD and he will sustain you; he will never let the righteous be shaken.

Centered on God

KIM TAYLOR HENRY

You surround me with songs of deliverance.

PSALM 32:7 (NASB)

I need to focus on God, I thought. *But how? How do I tune out the pain and tune in to God?* It was almost two weeks post-op. I was beginning to feel better, but nighttime was difficult. I could no longer tolerate narcotic pain medicine, and muscle spasms attacked my leg.

I put on my headphones and closed my eyes to Andrea Bocelli singing "The Lord's Prayer." I let every word sink in. Bocelli's voice was like an angel's, its splendor and richness a taste of heaven. I played the song over and over; I let it consume me. "For thine is the kingdom and the power and the glory forever." Bocelli's voice crescendoed, and so did my love for God. Instead of thinking about my pain, I concentrated on God's magnificence. I felt bathed in His love, enveloped by His peace. I wanted nothing more than to praise Him. In the midst of my praise, my weary body relaxed and I slept.

The next night, I found another song that, along with "The Lord's Prayer," carried me through my recovery. It was Melissa Greene's passionate rendition of "At Your Feet":

"Let the world fade away... Father find me now as I bow at your feet..."

This centering on God became my replacement for pain medicine. Through these songs, I abided in Him. As I did, not only the world but also my pain faded.

Let Us Pray

**Thank You, Lord, for the peace You give.
May I always abide in You.**

Further Reflection

PSALM 145:1–3 (NASB)

I will exalt You, my God, the King, And I will bless Your name forever and ever. Every day I will bless You, And I will praise Your name forever and ever. Great is the LORD, and highly to be praised; And His greatness is unsearchable.

Making Room

MARK COLLINS

*Then shall the virgin rejoice in the
dance, both young men and old together:
for I will turn their mourning into
joy, and will comfort them, and make
them rejoice from their sorrow.*

JEREMIAH 31:13 (KJV)

We live in the smallest house in the neighborhood.
Actually, we may live in the smallest house in several
neighborhoods. Sandee and I moved here BK (before kids)
and referred to our tiny abode as "our starter home." That was
twenty-five years and three kids ago. Whatever we were supposed to start is surely finished by now.

Five people in a small house is—well—intimate. I can hon-
estly say that I learned more about my daughters' daily habits
than I wanted to. I have seen my kids stand on the porch in a
driving rainstorm just to have privacy on the phone. Perhaps
I uttered some blue language while working on a car in the
driveway, only to have my kids—on the second floor, mind
you—chastise my swearing.

Now it's Christmas and they're all home again, plus some
out-of-town guests, so one or more kids will sleep on the floor
or couch. You'd think this would lead to conflicts, but it's

mostly (and surprisingly) peaceful. There is a lot of laughter, a lot of screaming (usually lyrics to the B-52s), a lot of what loosely would be labeled dancing.

And having survived on this small island for twenty-five years, isolated with four others in the primitive tribe, I happily join the natives in dance. Turns out, it doesn't require much space to make a family—couple of walls, really, or maybe a barn if there's no other place. I'm sure someone will sleep on the floor if that's what it takes to make room this season.

Let Us Pray

Lord, sometimes my home is crowded and my heart is not open. Let me learn how to make more room in both.

Further Reflection

ROMANS 12:16–18 (KJV)

Be of the same mind one toward another. Mind not high things, but condescend to men of low estate. Be not wise in your own conceits. Recompense to no man evil for evil. Provide things honest in the sight of all men. If it be possible, as much as lieth in you, live peaceably with all men.

Community of Song

RICK HAMLIN

O come, let us sing to the LORD; let us make a joyful noise to the rock of our salvation!

PSALM 95:1 (NRSV)

We were at an orphanage in a village in Kenya. We had come with friends from the United States who had raised money through their church to dig a well here.

We sat at a long table in a spare concrete-block room with a group of village dignitaries, waiting for lunch. Their English was good, but after twenty minutes, most of the nice-to-meet-you conversation topics were exhausted. Lunch was still heating up in the kitchen.

"Rick," the head of our group said to me, "why don't you lead us in a song?"

What song will everybody know? "Amazing Grace" was a safe bet. Everyone picked up the tune, some singing in Swahili, some in English.

"Let's do 'What a Friend We Have in Jesus,'" one woman suggested.

"Do you know 'Shall We Gather at the River?'" we asked. Someone fetched hymnbooks, and our repertoire expanded.

Our voices—young, old, Kenyan, American—echoed through the tin roof. The twenty-something Kenyan student sang a beautiful descant; the eighty-three-year-old former principal of the local school sang a baritone harmony. We learned new songs and they learned new songs, but time and again, we discovered we knew the same ones. At one point, the woman sitting next to me asked, "Where did you learn these hymns?"

"Probably the same place you learned them."

"In church?" she asked.

"Yes," I said.

How different our lives were. I lived in a place where fresh water was something we took for granted and flush toilets were hardly considered a luxury. She grew up here where a new well had changed lives dramatically, but our vocabulary of faith was exactly the same.

Let Us Pray

Music is Your gift to us, Lord. I sing my thanks and praise.

Further Reflection

ROMANS 12:4–5 (NRSV)

For as in one body we have many members, and not all the members have the same function, so we, who are many, are one body in Christ, and individually members one of another.

For the Love of Coffee

PAM KIDD

Sing to the Lord *with grateful praise.*

PSALM 147:7 (NIV)

My husband and I find ourselves in a hotel that misses criteria by a couple of stars. "It's convenient and the price is good," David points out. But the next morning, I'm congested and red-eyed, and David says he feels as if he's slept on a bed of rocks.

To be sure, no one's going to be bringing us coffee, so as David showers, I set out for salvation. I dash down the stairs, thinking, *Coffee!*—and almost collide with a man pushing a housekeeping cart.

"Good morning," he says. "And isn't it a fine day?" His enthusiasm startles me. There's something in his eyes. Contentment? In his warmth, my bad attitude melts like spring snow.

I squeeze out my first smile of the day. "Do you know where I might find coffee?"

"Oh yes, missy, there's a machine just down the hall."

As he points, I say, "Oh, great, I didn't bring money."

"Don't you worry," he says, digging in his pocket. "I always carry a little extra to help out folks."

Back in the room with two cups of tepid, watery coffee, I dig through my purse and come up with some cash to leave on a pillow. I scribble out a note of thanks, determined to put an even bigger smile on the man's face when he comes to clean our room.

Later, David and I sit in a trendy restaurant as the waiter serves us a special coffee blend, but I find this cup not half as good as my first one of the day.

Let Us Pray

Father, I see You in the eyes of a man pushing a cart, content. Let me exude that as well to those I meet along the way.

Further Reflection

PROVERBS 14:14 (NIV)

The faithless will be fully repaid for their ways, and the good rewarded for theirs.

PROVERBS 16:8 (NIV)

Better a little with righteousness than much gain with injustice.

Close in Nature

GAIL THORELL SCHILLING

Behold, I have given you
every herb bearing seed.

GENESIS 1:29 (KJV)

Grampy wasted nothing. In fact, he used words as frugally as he used bits of string, aluminum foil, and paper scraps. When we played checkers, he didn't chat. Nor do I remember him reading stories to me or speaking much at all besides saying, "Yup" and "Nope." But even with our very limited telegraph-style conversation, Grampy gave me a gift that has lasted all my life: he taught me to appreciate and identify wild plants.

While I was growing up in New Hampshire, Grampy lived with us, so when he rambled on walks along woodland paths, he often let me join him. I don't remember his holding my hand, but I do remember his pointing out various plants like a professional tour guide: "Lady's slipper." We'd squat down close so I could touch the bulbous pink flowers: "Checkerberry." He'd snap off a leathery leaf and chew it; I'd follow his example.

"It tastes like gum, Grampy."

"Yup. Wintergreen."

He pointed to tiny flowers with four pale petals—"Bluet"—and to vibrant red leaves—"Indian paintbrush." He carefully pulled aside serrated leaves to reveal where wild strawberries hid. He grasped a long cluster of wine-red berries dangling by a stone wall: "Chokeberry."

Choke? "Will I die if I taste, Grampy?"

"Nope."

Though Grampy was custodian of our church for years before I was born, I never saw him there. He once told me he didn't want to dress up to go. Perhaps he felt closer to God in the woodlands than around a lot of people. Grampy died when I was only twelve, but in those few years I spent with him, he taught me forever to cherish God's creation.

Let Us Pray

Creator God, in the tranquil beauty of growing things, I feel You are near.

Further Reflection

DEUTERONOMY 32:2 (KJV)

My doctrine shall drop as the rain, my speech shall distil as the dew, as the small rain upon the tender herb, and as the showers upon the grass.

ISAIAH 55:12 (NIV)

You will go out in joy and be led forth in peace; the mountains and hills will burst into song before you, and all the trees of the field will clap their hands.

Daddy's Got You

BROCK KIDD

*Your heavenly Father knoweth that ye
have need of all these things.*

MATTHEW 6:32 (KJV)

How am I going to keep doing this, God?" I shot the prayer up under my breath. The stock market had been frenetic, and the global economy was stoking the fire. My job as an investment adviser was to manage my clients' savings as well as their expectations. While I love what I do, sometimes the stress of it all becomes overwhelming. As the closing bell rang, I decided to call it a day.

At home, I was eager to spend a little time with our six-month-old baby girl. "Daddy's got you, Mary Katherine!" I swooped my daughter up in the air and smiled as I looked into her bright hazel eyes. She cooed back at me with a big, toothless grin. I could feel my stress melt away as she giggled and squealed. Before long, her happy cheer turned into a fussy whine. I knew this meant, "Daddy, I'm sleepy." It was nap time. I fed her a bottle and gently patted her back until she burped. Then I rocked her for a bit, and soon she was sound asleep.

"There are few things as peaceful as a sleeping baby," I said to my wife, Corinne, as I walked into the kitchen.

"So how was work?" she asked, sensing my weariness.

"Stressful."

She smiled and rolled her eyes. "Brock, you just spent an hour taking great care of Mary Katherine. God has been taking care of you for forty years! Do you think He is going to stop now?"

Suddenly, my burden felt a bit lighter. *Daddy's got you, Mary Katherine*, I thought to myself, *and my Father in heaven has me too.*

Let Us Pray

Father, sometimes even a grown-up needs a daddy. Thanks for being mine.

Further Reflection

PHILIPPIANS 4:19 (KJV)

But my God shall supply all your need according to his riches in glory by Christ Jesus.

1 JOHN 3:1 (NIV)

See what great love the Father has lavished on us, that we should be called children of God! And that is what we are! The reason the world does not know us is that it did not know him.

Never Flying Solo

CAROL KNAPP

And He will be the stability of your times.

ISAIAH 33:6 (NASB)

I'm not a fan of flying. It doesn't seem natural to be suspended miles in the sky. I fly because I have to. When you have family in Alaska, it's a bit of a drive from Minnesota. The night before I flew out to visit them, I prayed for peace, remembering how Jesus told His disciples: "Peace I leave with you" (John 14:27, NIV).

Everything went fine until I had to travel on a small commuter plane from Anchorage to Homer, situated on the Kenai Peninsula coastline. That day, a blizzard hit. The plane was delayed but flying.

When we boarded on the snowy runway, the young pilot stood by the steps to greet us. Someone asked how the weather was in Homer and if we'd be able to make a landing. Unbelievably, he replied, "Well, it's good enough to *try!*"

I have to get there, I thought, as I found my seat. Again I asked Jesus for His peace. At takeoff, the pilot informed us, "If we can't land in Homer, we're flying to Kodiak." *Kodiak Island!* I knew no one there. Besides this, we were told that several bags had been randomly removed to "make weight" and would arrive later.

We had a smooth flight above thick clouds. Homer had cleared, offering a breathless view of Kachemak Bay with its glistening mountains. A familiar green and black bag even popped up on the conveyor belt.

I fly because I have to ... because there are times when if I didn't need to ask God, I might never experience His perfect peace as I did on that trip.

Let Us Pray

**Lord of earth and sky, it's when I feel small
that I know I have a big God.**

Further Reflection

PSALM 119:165 (NASB)

Those who love Your Law have great peace, And nothing causes them to stumble.

Take a Break

BILL GIOVANNETTI

And Jesus answered and said to her,
"Martha, Martha, you are worried
and troubled about many things. But
one thing is needed, and Mary has
chosen that good part, which will not be
taken away from her."

LUKE 10:41–42 (NKJV)

I was excited to discover a host of online Bible reading plans, which promised an orderly way to finish the Bible in one year—a goal I value. My perfectionist tendencies can sometimes push me too hard with this, a little voice telling me I can't skip a day, can't fall behind in my reading. That voice sucks all the joy out of simply resting my heart in God's beautiful love letter.

After three weeks of daily readings, I logged in to my plan and was surprised to find this message: "No reading is

scheduled for today. Use today to take a break or to catch up on readings you missed."

For a moment, I didn't know what to do. My inner Martha jumped to high alert. *What do you mean, no reading today? I have to read! There are chapters to finish, verses to master, stories to study!*

Suddenly, a sense of peace washed over me. I took a deep breath and smiled. *It's OK, Martha. It's OK to rest. You don't have to work so hard, even for God. Take a break. Jesus is still with you.*

I set aside my laptop to play with my son. I had a wrestling match in my soul, but in the end, like Mary, I chose the good part.

Let Us Pray

**Lord, slow me down enough to be
good company for You.**

Further Reflection

LUKE 10:38–40 (NKJV)

Now it happened as they went that He entered a certain village; and a certain woman named Martha welcomed Him into her house. And she had a sister called Mary, who also sat at Jesus' feet and heard His word. But Martha was distracted with much serving, and she approached Him and said, "Lord, do You not care that my sister has left me to serve alone? Therefore tell her to help me."

Pointing toward Peace

EVELYN BENCE

When my spirit was overwhelmed
within me, Then You knew my path.

PSALM 142:3 (NKJV)

On her eighth birthday, my neighbor girl with special needs invited me to her family's celebration: cake, soda, and balloons. Five adults gathered around the table, sang the traditional song, and urged her to blow out the candles—eight thin stubs encircling a fat figure eight. With big brown eyes, she stared, silent as breath. Her mother, grandmother, and I coaxed. We modeled technique, blowing out one candle at a time. She laughed when her grandmother ran a finger through the icing and slathered it across her cheek. Still, the girl watched the burning candles, speechless, until finally an adult blew out the last flame. After lots of clapping, everyone ate big pieces of cake. A nice little party.

Or so I thought. Fifteen minutes later, she and I sat out on our shared front stoop. "That was a great birthday, wasn't it?"

"Yes," she stammered, "but I didn't get to blow out my candles."

"Were you afraid?" I asked.

"Yes. Too many people."

"Well, let's try again," I suggested.

Days later, it was my turn to feel unnerved; the week's demands overwhelmed me. When I heard the school bus brakes and watched my friend trudge into her day, I remembered our workable solution to her birthday dilemma of too many people, too much pressure. Identify the problem and bring a fearsome obstacle down to a manageable size. As I scaled back my to-do list, I made room for God's peace.

Let Us Pray

Lord, when my loved ones and I feel overwhelmed, help me see options that point us away from fear and toward peace.

Further Reflection

JAMES 3:18 (NKJV)

Now the fruit of righteousness is sown in peace by those who make peace.

Never Too Late

MARION BOND WEST

Be devoted to one another . . .
[as members of one family].

ROMANS 12:10 (AMP)

I sometimes brood about my mothering days when my children were young. Observing other mothers with their children now, I realize how simple it would have been to have bent over to their level more, hugged more, and said to each of them more often, "I love you."

Now I was certain it was too late.

Recently, my daughter Julie was going through a difficult day. As she left my house, we stood at the back door, saying goodbye. Suddenly, she threw her arms around me, and I grabbed her tight. "I love you, Mother."

"I love you too, Julie."

"It's so good to hear you say it, Mother."

"I thought you were too old." I tightened my grip.

Julie shed her tears openly.

Mine got stuck somewhere down inside of me.

"You didn't say it much when we were little," she whispered so softly I could have missed the words.

"Oh, I'm so sorry, Julie. Can you forgive me?" She nodded, unable to speak. "Thank you, Julie Babe."

"I want to hear them, Mother. I always did." Still holding my daughter, I spoke the words again. So did she. The powerful words went straight to my heart and rested there like a contented kitten.

Now, each time we end a telephone conversation or say goodbye in person, we add, "I love you," simultaneously.

Let Us Pray

Oh, my Father, I've neglected to speak the words
to You too. Thank You that it's never too late
to change. I love You. I love You.

Further Reflection

LUKE 6:31 (AMP)

Treat others the same way you want them to treat you.

EPHESIANS 4:32 (AMP)

Be kind and helpful to one another, tender-hearted [compassionate, understanding], forgiving one another [readily and freely], just as God in Christ also forgave you.

EPHESIANS 6:4 (AMP)

Fathers, do not provoke your children to anger [do not exasperate them to the point of resentment with demands that are trivial or unreasonable or humiliating or abusive; nor by showing favoritism or indifference to any of them], but bring them up [tenderly, with lovingkindness] in the discipline and instruction of the Lord.

Following His Example

SCOTT WALKER

By the seventh day God completed His work which He had done, and He rested on the seventh day from all His work . . . Then God blessed the seventh day and sanctified it.

GENESIS 2:2–3 (NASB)

In the Creation account of Genesis, God makes the world in six days and then rests on the seventh day. Not only does God rest, but He also sanctifies the seventh day of Creation for the purpose of recuperating from labor.

If there is anything that plagues modern-day folks, it is chronic fatigue. Seldom do we get enough sleep. And rare is the day when we truly disconnect from work and worry.

A second observation may sound a bit strange coming from a man who spent thirty-five years as a pastor: the church or synagogue often does not respect the mandate to rest on the Sabbath.

For people who have a Judeo-Christian heritage, the Sabbath is not only a time of rest but also a day of worship. As a pastor, I would often be up late on Saturday night, finishing my sermon and preparing for worship leadership. I would arrive early at the church on Sunday for the first of multiple services. I often taught a Sunday school class. Then, after lunch, I would attend committee meetings followed by an evening vespers service and Sunday night fellowship. Sunday was the most exhausting day of my week.

There is a need to regain balance on the equal claim of rest *and* worship on the Sabbath. Both must be experienced in fullness in order to retain spiritual and physical health.

Let Us Pray

Dear God, help me to know that if You need rest, I must rest too. Amen.

Further Reflection

MATTHEW 8:24 (NASB)

And behold, a violent storm developed on the sea, so that the boat was being covered by the waves; but Jesus Himself was asleep.

MARK 6:31 (NASB)

And He said to them, "Come away by yourselves to a secluded place and rest a little while." (For there were many people coming and going, and they did not even have time to eat.)

Be Choosy

BROCK KIDD

Peace, peace to him that is far off,
and to him that is near.

ISAIAH 57:19 (KJV)

My wife, Corinne, and I were going to extend a business
trip I had to make to Colorado and enjoy a few days of
vacation. I couldn't wait. The last year of my life had been more
than mind-boggling, and merging households and lifestyles had
proven to be more difficult than we thought it would be.

We had both been single and career-oriented for many
years. I had been raising Harrison, my eleven-year-old son;
Corinne had her career plus the new responsibility of creating a
home for someone other than herself. Our work schedules were
different, and we both had our own sets of friends. Sometimes
it seemed we were swimming upstream.

No wonder I had grabbed this time to take my fairly new
bride away from it all. After my meetings, I found myself alone
with Corinne. Acres of pure white powder covered a pristine

mountain; a big blue sky spread above us. The sparkling snow created an aura of simplicity and peace. I was reminded of why we had fallen in love. We wanted to create a life together, something good, worthwhile . . . a place of peace.

I thought ahead to the chaos of everyday life back in Nashville, Tennessee. We couldn't stay on this mountaintop forever, but we could create spaces of peace wherever we happened to be. Together, we needed to be choosier about the activities we took on, take turns with household chores, and create more family space. After all, there were sunsets waiting and chances for early-morning coffee, long talks, and night walks. The choice to move toward a life of peace would always be ours.

Let Us Pray

Father, give us the wisdom to search for and find Your perfect peace.

Further Reflection

1 THESSALONIANS 5:23–24 (KJV)

And the very God of peace sanctify you wholly; and I pray God your whole spirit and soul and body be preserved blameless unto the coming of our Lord Jesus Christ. Faithful is he that calleth you, who also will do it.

Right Now

JULIA ATTAWAY

*Elisha prayed, "Open his eyes,
LORD, so that he may see."*

2 KINGS 6:17 (NIV)

For the first time in months, I awoke before my alarm. The temperature had dropped. *Good morning, Lord. I love You,* I said silently. Then I went to make coffee.

I smiled as I walked into the kitchen of our new apartment. It is a separate room, not the mere three-foot-long stretch of counter adjacent to the living/dining area in our old place. I luxuriated in it, thankful, as I poured hot water into the French press and stirred the ground coffee with a chopstick. Then I padded across the new blue carpet to my chair in the living room. Early-morning sun glinted off the bricks of the apartment building across the street. Sparrows twittered somewhere. Life felt good.

I sipped my coffee and chuckled. Absolutely nothing was different that morning except the temperature and a good night's sleep. Every problem I'd had the day before still existed. One of my kids was in the hospital after a suicide attempt. Another was struggling mightily with the stress of the situation. Our prior landlord refused to return my calls to negotiate an end to our lease. Many things in my life were not good, yet I was feeling reasonably content.

I prayed (wryly): "You were right, Lord. Feeling helpless doesn't mean everything is hopeless." Fortunately, when I stress because I can't imagine a way out of a bad situation, God gently corrects my thoughts: *Right now*, I can't see the way. Perhaps tomorrow I will. I may wake up, smell the coffee, and see the light, and what felt impossible will feel more doable.

I can't always imagine that possibility. What I can do, though, is pray.

Let Us Pray

**Lord, teach me to trust in You more
than I trust my feelings.**

Further Reflection

PROVERBS 3:5–6 (NIV)

Trust in the LORD with all your heart and lean not on your own understanding; in all your ways submit to him, and he will make your paths straight.

No Bells, No Whistles

ERIKA BENTSEN

We are His workmanship, created in
Christ Jesus for good works, which
God prepared beforehand.

EPHESIANS 2:10 (NKJV)

I was going through cards you'd sent us over the years, which makes me thank you again for that coffeemaker you bought us last year," Mom said over the phone. "It works great."

I laughed. "It was hard to find one that only made coffee. Most of them came with too many features. You didn't need an alarm clock, an AM/FM radio, a milk steamer, or a data port. All you needed was a coffeemaker."

"Do you remember what you wrote when you sent it?"

I didn't, so Mom read it to me. "This gift is not fancy or expensive. No bells, no whistles, no distracting features. It does only one job but does it very well. It is efficient. There is no mistaking its purpose. May we all live up to its example."

I chuckled. "I write goofy cards."

"It's not goofy at all," Mom insisted. "Whenever I read this, I think about people unhappy with the way they look or with their natural talents. They exhaust themselves trying to be something they're not. We would be so much more at peace if we simply accepted how God made us and tried to be the best 'us' we could be."

I thought about the times I fought my Maker's plan before I accepted me for me. The wasted trips to the salon for the "right" hair, which was never right for me; wishing I were shorter; wishing I'd been born in England so I could have a cool accent.

Actually, I'd like most of all to be more like my mom—staid, solid, comfortable in being the wonderful person she is.

"You know, Mom, you're about the best coffeepot I've ever met."

"You, too, honey. You too." *Not yet, but maybe someday.*

Let Us Pray

Lord, please give me satisfaction in Your purpose for me so I will fit into the artwork of life You designed.

Further Reflection

DEUTERONOMY 14:2 (NKJV)

For you are a holy people to the LORD your God, and the LORD has chosen you to be a people for Himself, a special treasure above all the peoples who are on the face of the earth.

JOHN 1:3 (NKJV)

All things were made through Him, and without Him nothing was made that was made.

Author Index

A Note from the Editors

We hope you enjoyed *Held in Perfect Peace*, published by Guideposts. For over 75 years, Guideposts, a nonprofit organization, has been driven by a vision of a world filled with hope. We aspire to be the voice of a trusted friend, a friend who makes you feel more hopeful and connected.

By making a purchase from Guideposts, you join our community in touching millions of lives, inspiring them to believe that all things are possible through faith, hope, and prayer. Your continued support allows us to provide uplifting resources to those in need. Whether through our communities, websites, apps, or publications, we inspire our audiences, bring them together, and comfort, uplift, entertain, and guide them. Visit us at guideposts.org to learn more.

We would love to hear from you. Write us at Guideposts, P.O. Box 5815, Harlan, Iowa 51593 or call us at (800) 932-2145. Did you love *Held in Perfect Peace*? Leave a review for this product on guideposts.org/shop. Your feedback helps others in our community find relevant products.

Find inspiration, find faith, find Guideposts.

Shop our best sellers and favorites at

guideposts.org/shop

From the Publisher

GREAT BOOKS

ARE EVEN BETTER WHEN THEY'RE SHARED!

Help other readers find this one:

- Post a review at your favorite online bookseller

- Post a picture on a social media account and share why you enjoyed it

- Send a note to a friend who would also love it—or better yet, give them a copy

Thanks for reading!